What Do Your FLOWERS Say Today?

SUE ADAMS

Balboa Press books may be ordered through booksellers or by contacting:

Balboa Press
A Division of Hay House
1663 Liberty Drive
Bloomington, IN 47403
www.balboapress.com
844-682-1282

Edited by Becky Adams

ISBN: 978-1-9822-5373-8 (sc)
ISBN: 978-1-9822-5374-5 (e)

Library of Congress Control Number: 2020916328

Print information available on the last page.

Balboa Press rev. date: 09/29/2020

BALBOA.PRESS
A DIVISION OF HAY HOUSE

DEDICATION

This book is dedicated to my family, who brings me even more joy than the flowers that surround me.

To my mother and father who instilled confidence, taught me the value of hard work, and always encouraged me in my endeavors. To my daughter Becky, a wonderful editor, and a daughter I am very proud of. To my son-in-law Michael for his eager approval of all my endeavors. To my granddaughters Ambika and Priya, for their love and enthusiasm. To my husband Mark, who supports, encourages and loves me. To my sisters Deanna and Margaret, who have attended many, many flower readings, for their love and support.

I would also like to thank Margery Daughtrey, Senior Extension Associate, Cornell University, who, when I told her of my research and ideas, said, "Brilliant! Get published!" Also, thanks to Neil Mattson, Associate Professor, Cornell University, for his support and enthusiasm for this project. Photos were integral to this book. Thanks to Ball Horticulture Company, Proven Winners, A.D.R. Bulbs, Margery Daughtrey, Maryanne Pool of Maryanne's Floral Garden, the floral and marketing departments of Adams Fairacre Farms, Bill Miller, Cornell University Professor of Plant Science and Aneta Ferreira, Plainview Growers.

INTRODUCTION

Flowers are a great source of energy and inspiration. We use them to express love, sympathy, friendship, congratulations, and well wishes. Flowers are an integral part of rituals and rites of passage, such as weddings, funerals, births, baptisms, and dedications. When we choose flowers for the events in our lives, do we stop to think about what the individual blooms mean?

Flowers have meanings – the type of flower, color, shape, and number of petals all have significance. The idea of this book is to help unlock those meanings so that you can use flowers as a tool to provide inner guidance and wisdom.

At one time, flower meanings were part of the lexicon of society. Certain flowers have served as symbols since ancient times. The Egyptians used the lotus flower to represent the sun, creation, and rebirth. The lotus opens in the morning and closes at night – it is "reborn" with each sunrise. Some flowers, like narcissus, which represents egotism, derive their meanings from myths. The meanings of other flowers come from their appearance, such as the Bird of Paradise, which looks like the head and beak of a tropical bird, hence the meaning of paradise, or joy.

The study of the meaning of flowers is known as floriography. The Victorian era represented the height of floriography, as lovers would use flowers to send secret messages to each other. Victorians enjoyed attaching meaning to flowers, and would often wear them as symbols. The violet, for example, is a symbol of modesty and fidelity, and was particularly popular during this era. Oscar Wilde, the Victorian playwright, caused quite a stir when he encouraged his audience to wear a green carnation to the premier of *Lady Windemere's Fan*. He cleverly told them that it represented being a fan of Oscar Wilde.

Flowers not only have meanings, but they also make us feel good. Flower essences can help us feel better. Lavender, for example, is often used in aromatherapy to help us relax and manage stress. Dr. Edward Bach, an English homeopath in the 1930s, established a process of healing with flowers. Bach believed that illness resulted from a conflict between the soul's purpose and the personality's actions and outlook. This internal war, according to Bach, led to negative moods and energy blocking, thought to cause a lack of internal harmony that would lead to disease. His flower essences continue to gain popularity today, and demonstrate that we are naturally drawn to flowers for their healing energies.

I became interested in flower meanings when preparing for a talk about using color in combination planters I was to give to horticulture professionals at Cornell Field Days in 2010. Flower color research and flower meanings seemed to go hand in hand. I continued researching after the talk, and read about flower fortune telling. What a great topic for the seminars I was to give in the winter, I thought! So I committed to two seminars. Being co-owner of a 5-acre greenhouse business with a poinsettia crop to sell, I put this project aside until the end of December. When I googled flower fortune telling, all that came up were fortune tellers. It looked like I was on my own on this project. I carried a huge pile of Victorian books with me on the plane to our vacation in Australia, determined to figure out my presentation. To my dismay, I found out that flowers have many meanings by many different authors. This was not going to be an easy endeavor. When I reached Australia, I still hadn't figured out flower fortune telling. However, I had an epiphany on the return flight, deciding to conduct readings similar to angel cards, where instead of three cards, participants would choose three flowers. The flower readings I did for groups helped to refine my own flower meanings. I added shape, petal, and color information to make the readings more meaningful. Everyone enjoyed these events and often asked me to return. To expand my audience, I decided to write this book so that many more can benefit from what flowers have to say.

I hope that this book will encourage you to enjoy real flowers and to feel a greater connection to them. Flowers really do make us feel good and give off positive energy. When out looking at gardens and checking out your local florist, don't worry about the meanings – they grow to give us pleasure. And if you are drawn to one, that's the flower you need.

HOW TO USE THIS BOOK

A flower reading is a fun and enjoyable way to answer questions, receive guidance, and nourish our souls. When you are attracted to a particular flower, that's the flower whose healing energy you need. Each aspect of the flower, from the number of the petals, the color, to the flower's meaning (or meanings) will provide insight and inspire you to fulfill your hopes and dreams. Nature nurtures and flowers delight.

To create your flower reading:

1. Begin by looking at the flower photos. Which flowers are you particularly attracted to at this very moment? The flowers that you are drawn to tell a story of past, present, and future events, and will help you to move forward on the right path with their help.
2. Choose three flowers and write them in the order they were chosen. Pick a color for each of the flowers. The first flower represents the immediate past, the second the present, and the third a possible outcome.
3. Go to the page giving information about the first flower you chose. You'll see that the flower's details such as shape, color, and number of petals are all important elements that contribute to your reading. Repeat this process with your second and third flower choices.

To create a simple reading:

Choose one flower and see what message it has to share with you. This is a great way to start your day!

As you peruse this book, you will see that there are different meanings for the color, number of petals, and shape of the flower. This is because, like the flowers, colors, shapes, and numbers have multiple meanings. A message is offered for each flower, but you may find that by studying each aspect of the flower plus its meanings, you may come up with a more personal message.

Flowers have healing energy, which means color meanings and messages are generally positive. If meanings that resonate with you appear negative, keep in mind that you can often turn things around or prevent a disaster by changing your outlook and approach to a situation.

With flowers, fresh is best. The flowers that catch your eye in a garden or at a floral display will resonate more deeply than photos, although certainly both have value. People who look at flowers every day are happier and more successful, so the simple act of seeking out fresh flowers can provide you with a beneficial healing energy.

Flowers are a gift of beauty. Relax and relish the beautiful photos. Have fun creating flower readings. Flowers are magical and inspire us to reach our potential.

Alstroemeria

Lavender   White
Orange   Yellow
Pink
Purple
Red

Alstroemeria Inca Ice
* Ball Horticultural Company

Amaryllis

Orange
Pink
Red
White
Yellow

Amaryllis Double Dragon
* A.D.R. Bulbs

Anemone

Pink
Purple
Red
White

Anemone Mona Lisa Deep Blue Improved
* Ball Horticultural Company

Aster

Blue   White
Lavender
Pink
Purple
Red

Aster Blue Dragon
* Ball Horticultural Company

Astilbe

Lavender
Pink
Red
White

Astilbe Milk & Honey
* Ball Horticultural Company

Astrantia

Green
Pink
Purple
Red
White

Astrantia Rosea
* Ball Horticultural Company

Baby's Breath

White

Gypsophila
° Margery Daughtrey

Begonia

Orange
Pink
Red
White
Yellow

Begonia Prelude Plus Rose
° Ball Horticultural Company

Bell Flower (Campanula)

Blue
Pink
Purple
White

Anemone Mona Lisa Deep Blue Improved
° Ball Horticultural Company

Bells of Ireland

Green

Moluccella Bells of Ireland
° Ball Horticultural Company

Bird of Paradise

Bird of Paradise
° Tara Tornello, Adams Fairarce Farms

Black-eyed Susan (Rudbeckia)

Bronze
Gold

Rudbeckia Pot of Gold
° Ball Horticultural Company

Calla Lily

Black   White

Green   Yellow

Orange

Pink

Purple

Calla Amethyst
® Ball Horticultural Company

Carnation (Dianthus)

Dark Red   Striped

Light Red   Yellow

Pink

Purple

Dianthus Oscar Pink
® Ball Horticultural Company

Chrysanthemum

Red

Violet

White

Yellow

Garden Mum Cheryl Jolly Red
® Ball Horticultural Company

Cleome

Pink

Purple

White

Cleome Sparkler Mix
® Ball Horticultural Company

Coleus

Black

Green

Orange

Pink

Red

Coleus Wizard Mix
® Ball Horticultural Company

Columbine (Aquilegia)

Blue   Salmon

Pink   White

Purple   Yellow

Red

Aquilegia Earlybird Red Yellow
® Ball Horticultural Company

Coneflower (Echinacea)

Orange

Pink

Purple

Yellow

Echinacea PowWow Wild Berry
® Ball Horticultural Company

Coral Bells (Heuchera)

Bronze	Red
Green	Silver
Orange	
Purple	

Heuchera Cherry Cola
® Ball Horticultural Company

Coreopsis

Gold

Mango

Pink

Yellow

Coreopsis Double the Sun
® Ball Horticultural Company

Crocus

Blue	Yellow
Lavender	
Orange	
Purple	
White	

Crocus Ruby Giant
® A.D.R. Bulbs

Daffodil

Orange

White

Yellow

Daffodil Carlton
® A.D.R. Bulbs

Dahlia

Bronze	Yellow
Orange	
Pink	
Purple	
Red	

Dahlietta Lily
® Ball Horticultural Company

Daisy
(Leucanthemum)

Pink
White
Yellow

Leucanthemum Madonna
° Ball Horticultural Company

Dandelion

Yellow

Dandelion
°Sue Adams

Delphinium
(Larkspur)

Blue
Pink
Purple
White

Delphinium Guardian Blue
° Ball Horticultural Company

Forget-me-not
(Myosotis)

Blue
Pink
White

Myosotis Mon Amie Blue
° Ball Horticultural Company

Foxglove (Digitalis)

Blue
Pink
Purple
White

Digitalis Polkadot Priness
° Ball Horticultural Company

Freesia

Orange   Yellow
Pink
Purple
Red
White

Freesia Reiman Gardens
° A.D.R. Bulbs

Geranium

Orange
Pink
Purple
Red
White

Zonal Geranium Dynamo Salmon
° Ball Horticultural Company

Gerbera Daisy

Orange   Yellow
Pink
Purple
Red
White

Gerbera ColorBloom Yellow Dark Eye
° Ball Horticultural Company

Gladiola (Gladiolus)

Burgundy   Yellow
Pink
Purple
Red
White

Gladiolus Summer Sparkles
° Ball Horticultural Company

Golden Aster, Goldenrod (Solidago)

Yellow

Solidago Little Lemon
° Ball Horticultural Company

Heather (Calluna)

Pink
Purple
Red
White

Calluna
° Margery Daughtrey

Hellebore (Helleborus)

Black   White
Green   Yellow
Pink
Purple
Red

Helleborus Red Mountain
° Ball Horticultural Company

Hibiscus

Orange   Yellow
Peach
Pink
Purple
Red

Hibiscus Luna Pink Swirl
° Ball Horticultural Company

Hyacinth

Blue
Purple
White

Hyacinth Delft Blue
° A.D.R. Bulbs

Hydrangea

Blue
Pink
White

Let's Dance®Blue Jangles Reblooming Hydrangea
°Courtesy of Proven Winners provenwinners.com

Iris

Black   Purple
Blue   Red
Brown   White
Orange   Yellow
Pink

Iris Ruffled Velvet
° Ball Horticultural Company

Kangaroo Paw (Anigozanthos

Apricot
Orange
Pink
Red

Anigozanthos Red Pot-A-Roo
° Ball Horticultural Company

Lantana

Orange
Pink
Red
White
Yellow

Lucious® Royale Red Zone
°Sue Adams

11

Lavender
(Lavandula)

Pink

Purple

White

Sweet Romance® Lavender
®Courtesy of Proven Winners provenwinners.com

Liatris

Pink

Purple

White

Liatris floristan Violet
® Ball Horticultural Company

Lilac

Blue	Violet
Lilac	White
Magenta	
Pink	
Purple	

Lilac
®Margery Daughtrey

Lily

Orange

Pink

Red

White

Yellow

Asiatic Lily Assortment
® Ball Horticultural Company

Lisianthus

Black	White
Brown	
Green	
Lavender	
Pink	

Lisianthus ABC 1 Deep Rose
® Ball Horticultural Company

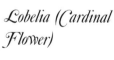

Lobelia (Cardinal
Flower)

Blue

Red

White

Yellow

Lobelia Vulcan Red
® Ball Horticultural Company

Lupine (Lupin)

Pink

Purple

Red

White

Yellow

Lupin Gallery Mini Blue Bicolor
° Ball Horticultural Company

Marigold

Gold

Orange

Red

Yellow

French Marigold Durango Gold
° Ball Horticultural Company

Million Bells (Calibrachoa)

Blue	Red
Orange	White
Pink	Yellow
Purple	

Superbells°Pink Calibrachoa
°Courtesy of Proven Winners provenwinners.com

Narcissus

White

Yellow

Narcissus
° A.D.R. Bulbs

Nasturtium

Orange

Pink

Red

White

Yellow

Nasturtium Baby Rose
° Ball Horticultural Company

Orchid

Green	White
Orange	Yellow
Pink	
Purple	
Red	

Orchid
° Aneta Ferreira, Photographer at Plainview Growers

Pansy

Blue   Yellow
Orange
Purple
Red
White

Pansy Cool Wave Mix
° Ball Horticultural Company

Petunia

Black   Salmon
Blue   White
Pink
Purple
Red

Supertunia Vista° Bubblegum
°Courtesy of Proven Winners provenwinners.com

Phlox

Pink
Purple
White

Phlox Gisele Pink
° Ball Horticultural Company

Poppy (Papaver)

Orange   Yellow
Pink
Purple
Red
White

Papaver Beauty Livermore
° Ball Horticultural Company

Queen Anne's Lace

White

Queen Anne's Lace
°Sue Adams

Ranunculus

Orange
Pink
Red
White
Yellow

Ranunculus Magic Mix
° Ball Horticultural Company

Rose

Burgundy	Pink
Cream	Purple
Dark Pink	Red
Green	Salmon
Lavender	White
Light Pink	Yellow
Peach	Orange

Hybrid Tea Rose Olympiad Macauck
° Ball Horticultural Company

Snapdragon

Orange	Violet
Peach	White
Pink	Yellow
Purple	
Red	

Cut Flower Snapdragon Potomac Light Rose
° Ball Horticultural Company

St. John's Wort (Hypericum)

Green
Peach
Red
Yellow

Hypericum
°Margery Daughtrey

Stock (Matthiola)

Lilac
Magenta
Pink
White
Yellow

Matthiola Opera Debora
° Ball Horticultural Company

Sunflower

Orange
Red
Yellow

Sunflower Miss Sunshine
° Ball Horticultural Company

Thistle (Eryngium)

Blue
Pink
White

Eryngium Blue Glitter
° Ball Horticultural Company

Tulip

Orange	Yellow
Purple	
Red	
Striped	
White	

Tulip Temple of Beauty
° A.D.R. Bulbs

Verbena

Blue
Pink
Purple
Red
White

Verbena Firehouse White
° Ball Horticultural Company

Violet (Viola)

Blue	Yellow
Pink	
Purple	
Violet	
White	

Viola Celestial Northern Lights
° Ball Horticultural Company

Wax Flower (Chamelaucium)

Pink
Purple
White
Yellow

Chamelaucium
°Sue Adams

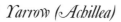

Yarrow (Achillea)

Orange
Pink
Red
White
Yellow

Achillea Moonshine
° Ball Horticultural Company

Zinnia

Orange	White
Pink	Yellow
Purple	
Red	
Salmon	

Zinnia Profusion 4 Colors Mix
° Ball Horticultural Company

ALSTROMERIA

3 petals
Shape: Star

Shape meaning: The star encourages us to evaluate ourselves and our lives. We strive to arrive at healthy conclusions so that we can go beyond ourselves and contribute to the larger world in the form of art, writing, political, or humanitarian action.

Number meaning: The spiritual energies of the number three activates positive thoughts, promoting efficacious energies and opportunities.

Color meanings
Lavender: Encourages us to be nurturing, and to give priority to the needs of others.

Orange: The color of encouragement, orange conveys excitement, warmth, and enthusiasm, keeping us motivated to look on the bright side of life. Orange stimulates action, encouraging us to seek out new activities and adventures.

Pink: Puts us in touch with our nurturing side, helping us to show tenderness and kindness with empathy and sensitivity. Pink seeks appreciation, respect, and admiration, and doesn't like to be taken for granted. Loves to hear the words "thank you."

Purple: Represents wisdom and spirituality. An introspective color, purple allows us to connect with our deeper thoughts and inspires us to reach our highest ideals.

Red: An energizing color, red excites the emotions, boosts enthusiasm, and urges us to take action.

White: In color psychology, white represents a new beginning, or a blank canvas. This is the time to seize new opportunities. White is reflective and stimulates openness, growth, and creativity.

Yellow: A great communicator, yellow loves to talk and helps with networking.

Flower meanings: Friendship, devotion, wealth, prosperity, fortune, survival, symbol for following your dreams

Flower message: Look to friends to help you overcome challenges so that you can achieve success in your endeavors.

AMARYLLIS

3 petals
Shape: Trumpet

Shape meaning: The trumpet shape indicates that news is coming your way.

Number meaning: The spiritual energies of the number three activates positive thoughts, promoting efficacious energies and opportunities.

Color Meanings
Orange: Social and inviting, orange is the color of the extrovert, exuding happiness and joy, and releasing inhibitions.

Pink: Puts us in touch with our nurturing side, helping us to show tenderness and kindness with empathy and sensitivity. Pink seeks appreciation, respect, and admiration, and doesn't like to be taken for granted. Loves to hear the words "thank you."

Red: An energizing color, red excites the emotions, boosts enthusiasm, and urges us to take action.

White: In color psychology, white represents a new beginning, or a blank canvas. This is the time to seize new opportunities. White is reflective and stimulates openness, growth, and creativity.

Yellow: A practical thinker, not a dreamer, yellow loves a challenge, especially a mental one, and will help find new ways of doing things. Yellow stimulates our mental faculties and inspires original thought and inquisitiveness.

Flower meanings: Pride, beauty

Flower message: "If you've got it, flaunt it!" You can be strong and self-confident. Like the amaryllis flower which blooms for a long time, the road to success may be long and difficult, but achievable.

ANEMONE

2 petals
Shape: Cup

Shape meaning: Cups are nurturing and embracing. In tarot cards, the cups can render messages of completion, expansion, abundance, and vibrancy. One's "cup of tea" is an expression that is used to describe something one enjoys or is good at.

Number meaning: Two reflects the quiet power of judgment and the need for planning. Two beckons us to choose and encourages partnerships and communication.

Color meanings
Pink: Creates a calming effect on our emotional energies and can relieve feelings of anger, aggression, and neglect. Pink represents compassion, nurturing, and love and shows tenderness with empathy and sensitivity.

Purple: Combines the stability and integrity of the color blue with the energy of red to promote harmony of the mind and emotions, contributing to mental balance.

Red: A strong-willed color, red increases confidence, especially to those who are shy or lacking in willpower, by providing a sense of security and protection against fear and anxiety.

White: The color of protection, white offers a sense of peace and calm, comfort and hope. Surrounding our aura with white light helps to deter negativity and encourages us see beyond surface emotions, entanglements, and fear.

Flower meanings: Forsaken, abandonment, anticipation

Flower message: Work through fears and sorrows. The anemone closes at night and opens in the morning, anticipating the new day. Something special is around the corner, no matter how dark things may look now.

ASTER

21 petals
Shape: Star

Shape meaning: The star encourages us to evaluate ourselves and our lives. We strive to arrive at healthy conclusions so that we can go beyond ourselves and contribute to the larger world in the form of art, writing, political, or humanitarian action.

Number meaning: Twenty-one symbolizes new beginnings. A chapter in your life will soon be ending, so look forward to another one beginning.

Color meanings

Blue: The shade of the sea and the sky, blue is often described as peaceful, secure, and orderly. The color of trust, blue is thought to induce calm and convey tranquility, helping to instill confidence, and inner security.

Lavender: Encourages us to daydream and galvanize our creative tendencies. Lavender helps us to be open to new thoughts and ideas.

Pink: A combination of red and white, pink combines the need for action of red with the insight offered by white to help us succeed.

Purple: Represents wisdom and spirituality. An introspective color, purple allows us to connect with our deeper thoughts and inspires us to reach for our highest ideals.

Red: Indicates that we need to be more creative and showy in our endeavors. Red encourages us to move forward. Now may be the time to pursue something we desire.

White: Considered a powerful color in feng shui, white creates a sense of order and efficiency, enabling us to declutter our lives of material items or emotional baggage.

Flower meanings: Daintiness, love, variety, beauty in retirement, cheerfulness in old age, unexpected surprise, patience, charm

Flower message: The star-like shape of the aster with its multitude of petals speaks of tiny beginnings from which all great things proceed. Little blessings will end with a pleasant surprise.

ASTILBE

Shape: Pyramid

Shape meaning: To the Greeks, the triangle is seen as the delta glyph and symbolizes a doorway. Balancing thought and emotion provides a doorway to higher wisdom.

Color meanings

Lavender: Encourages us to be nurturing, and to give priority to the needs of others.

Pink: Creates a calming effect on our emotional energies and can relieve feelings of anger, aggression, and neglect. Pink represents compassion, nurturing, and love, and shows tenderness with empathy and sensitivity.

Red: Indicates that we need to be more creative and showy in our endeavors. Red encourages us to move forward. Now may be the time to pursue something we desire.

White: Associated with being pure, fresh and good, white's basic feature is equality, implying fairness and impartiality, and reflecting the energies of truth. White urges us to reflect on past transgressions, ours or those of others, not to judge, but to understand, so that we can blossom into our higher selves.

Flower meanings: I'll still be waiting, love at first sight, worldly pleasures, patience, dedication

Flower message: Have patience with a loved one.

ASTRANTIA

5 petals
Shape: Star

Shape meaning: The star encourages us to evaluate ourselves and our lives. We strive to arrive at healthy conclusions so that we can go beyond ourselves and contribute to the larger world in the form of art, writing, political, or humanitarian action.

Number meaning: Five is the pivotal number of movement and change. Five is about enjoying life, trying new experiences, and making important choices.

Color meanings
Green: Puts heart and emotions in balance, helping to see both sides of the equation before making the appropriate decision.

Pink: In color psychology, pink is a sign of hope, a positive color that inspires warm and comforting feelings. Everything will be okay, or "everything will be rosy."

Purple: Represents wisdom and spirituality. An introspective color, purple allows us to connect with our deeper thoughts and inspires us to reach for high ideals.

Red: An energizing color, red excites the emotions, boosts enthusiasm, and urges us to take action.

White: The color of protection, white offers a sense of peace and calm, comfort and hope. Surrounding our aura with white light helps to deter negativity and encourages us see beyond surface emotions, entanglements, and fear.

Flower meanings: Strength, courage, protection

Flower message: You can achieve success if you have the courage to move forward.

BABY'S BREATH

5 petals
Shape: Ball

Shape meaning: A ball depicts courage, strength, and the confidence to face life's challenges.

Number meaning: Five is the pivotal number of movement and change. Five is about enjoying life, trying new experiences, and making important choices.

Color Meaning
White: The color of protection, white offers a sense of peace and calm, comfort and hope. Surrounding our aura with white light helps to deter negativity and encourages us see beyond surface emotions, entanglements, and fear.

Flower meaning: Happiness, purity of heart, innocence, self-discipline

Flower message: Stay dedicated to your cause and remember the power of innocence. Proceed with confidence, but be modest.

BEGONIA

3 petals
Shape: Cup

Shape meaning: The cup shape indicates we are thinking with our hearts instead of our heads, thus reflecting spontaneous responses and habitual reactions to situations.

Number meaning: The spiritual energies of the number three activates positive thoughts, promoting efficacious energies and opportunities.

Color meanings
Orange: Social and inviting, orange encourages two-way conversations.

Pink: Puts us in touch with our nurturing side, helping us to show tenderness and kindness with empathy and sensitivity. Pink seeks appreciation, respect, and admiration, and doesn't like to be taken for granted. Loves to hear the words "thank you."

Red: A strong-willed color, red increases confidence, especially to those who are shy or lacking in willpower, by providing a sense of security and protection against fear and anxiety.

White: The color of protection, white offers a sense of peace and calm, comfort and hope. Surrounding our aura with white light helps to deter negativity and encourages us see beyond surface emotions, entanglements, and fear.

Yellow: Puts emotions aside so thoughts come from the head rather than the heart to help with making decisions. Like a scientist who constantly analyzes and looks methodically at both sides, yellow helps us to focus, study, and recall information.

Flower meanings: Warning, dark thoughts, caution regarding new situations, gratitude and giving thanks for a favor from someone else

Flower message: The begonia's symbolism is a call to be more watchful. It's not about panic or fear. Since the naming of the flower was a tribute to a helpful official, be sure to show thanks to those who help you along the way.

BELLFLOWER (CAMPANULA)

5 petals
Shape: Bell or cup

Shape meaning: Cups are nurturing and embracing. In tarot cards, the cups can render messages of completion, expansion, abundance and vibrancy. One's "cup of tea" is an expression that is used to describe something one enjoys or is good at. The bell shape indicates that guidance from within (our intuition) needs to be grounded and put into practice.

Number meaning: Five is the pivotal number of movement and change. Five is about enjoying life, trying new experiences, and making important choices.

Color meanings
Blue: The shade of the sea and the sky, blue is often described as peaceful, secure, and orderly. The color of trust, blue is thought to induce calm and convey tranquility, helping to instill confidence and inner security.

Pink: A combination of red and white, pink combines the need for action of red with the insight offered by white to help us succeed.

Purple: Assists those seeking the meaning of life and spiritual fulfillment. Purple enhances psychic ability but at the same time keeps us grounded.

White: The color of protection, white offers a sense of peace and calm, comfort and hope. Surrounding our aura with white light helps to deter negativity and encourages us see beyond surface emotions, entanglements, and fear.

Flower meaning: Humility, constancy, delicate and lonely as this flower, thankfulness, gratitude, aspiring

Flower message: Be yourself, don't let yourself be judged by outside influences. Choose your path and head directly towards it.

BELLS OF IRELAND

5 petals
Shape: Bell

Shape meaning: The bell shape indicates that guidance from within (our intuition) needs to be grounded and put into practice.

Number meaning: Five is the pivotal number of movement and change. Five is about enjoying life, trying new experiences, and making important choices.

Color meaning
Green: A refreshing and peaceful color, green evokes a feeling of abundance. In nature we see green in all its glory, expressing renewal and life.

Flower meaning: Good luck, prosperity

Flower message: Luck is coming your way!

BIRD OF PARADISE

3 petals
Shape: Resembles a bird in flight

Shape meaning: This flower resembles a bird in flight, encouraging us to take action towards a desire.

Number meaning: The spiritual energies of the number three activates positive thoughts, promoting efficacious energies and opportunities.

Color meanings
Blue: The shade of the sea and the sky, blue is often described as peaceful, secure, and orderly. The color of trust, blue is thought to induce calm and convey tranquility, helping to instill confidence and inner security.

Orange: The color of encouragement, orange conveys excitement, warmth, and enthusiasm, keeping us motivated to look on the bright side of life. Orange stimulates action, encouraging us to seek out new activities and adventures.

Yellow: Represents youth, fun, joy, sunshine, and happy feelings. Yellow is also a symbol of friendship, new beginnings, and happiness.

Flower meanings: Magnificence, something strange and wonderful is about to occur, joyfulness, wonderful anticipation

Flower message: Stay open to new possibilities. Explore the world with a sense of optimism and excitement.

BLACK-EYED SUSAN (RUDBECKIA)

5 petals
Shape: Circle

Shape meaning: The circle evokes the idea of movement and symbolizes the cycle of time.

Number meaning: Five is the pivotal number of movement and change. Five is about enjoying life, trying new experiences, and making important choices.

Color Meanings
Bronze: Intimately related to nature, bronze encourages growth through experience.

Gold: Associated with richness in life or spirit, gold enhances the true self and helps develop the psyche. Gold helps to cope with any task, and upon completion, will showcase our capabilities.

Flower meanings Justice, impartiality, encouragement, motivation, renewal, completion

Flower message: The arrow-shaped leaves are pointing to something that is hidden around you. Is there something you are ignoring? This flower has the energy to awaken insight. There is a need for change, but it must be initiated properly.

CALLA LILY

1 petal
Shape: Trumpet

Shape meaning: The trumpet indicates that news is coming your way.

Number meaning: The number one represents new beginnings and fresh starts. Don't be tied to past mistakes. You're entering a new phase, starting over with a clean slate.

Color meanings
Black: Creates a grounding effect on our environment when used sparingly.

Green: A refreshing and peaceful color, green has a strong association with nature, helping us to relax and relieve stress.

Orange: Orange is the color of bright sunsets, so many associate the color orange with beauty.

Pink: Puts us in touch with our nurturing side, helping us to show tenderness and kindness with empathy and sensitivity. Pink seeks appreciation, respect, and admiration, and doesn't like to be taken for granted. Loves to hear the words "thank you."

Purple: Represents wisdom and spirituality. An introspective color, purple allows us to connect with our deeper thoughts and inspires us to reach for our highest ideals.

White: Considered a powerful color in feng shui, white creates a sense of order and efficiency, enabling us to declutter our lives of material items or emotional baggage.

Yellow: Represents youth, fun, joy, sunshine, and happy feelings. Yellow is also a symbol of friendship, new beginnings, and happiness.

Flower meaning: Magnificent beauty, majesty, modesty, youth and rebirth, victory

Flower message: Focus on the beauty around you. Nature nurtures.

CARNATION (DIANTHUS)

5 to 40 petals
Shape: Circle

Shape meaning: The circle evokes the idea of movement and symbolizes the cycle of time.

Number meaning: The number five represents adventure and freedom, encouraging us to embrace new experiences.

Color Meanings
Unlike other flowers in this book, carnations have specific meanings for their colors, and they are included here.

Pink: Represents sweet and innocent children, or our inner child. Pink symbolizes uncomplicated emotions, inexperience, and naivety, and stands for unconditional love and understanding. Pink can bring back pleasant childhood memories associated with the care and thoughtfulness of a maternal figure. The pink carnation represents Mother's love and gratitude.

Purple: Represents wisdom and spirituality. An introspective color, purple allows us to connect with our deeper thoughts and inspires us to reach for our highest ideals. A purple carnation represents capriciousness.

Light Red: An energizing color, red excites the emotions, boosts enthusiasm and urges us to take action. The light red carnation represents admiration.

Dark Red: We may be overextending ourselves. Be careful about how we expend our physical energies. Dark red carnations represent love and affection.

Striped: Refusal.

Yellow: Puts emotions aside so thoughts come from the head rather than the heart to help with making decisions. Like a scientist who constantly analyzes and looks methodically at both sides, yellow helps us to focus, study, and recall information. The yellow carnation represents disappointment, rejection.

Flower meanings, general: Make haste, love, mother's love, fascination, pride, beauty, devotion

Flower message: Don't hesitate to take the next step to initiate and strengthen relationships.

CHRYSANTHEMUM

Number of petals depends on variety
Shape: Circle

Shape meaning: The circle evokes an idea of movement and symbolizes the cycle of time.

Color meanings
Unlike other flowers in this book, chrysanthemums have specific meanings for their colors, and they are included here.

Red: A warm color, red, evokes a strong sense of passion. The red chrysanthemum represents love and deep passion.

Violet: Wisdom, combined with sensitivity, makes violet capable of helping those in need. Violet chrysanthemum means "wishes to get well."

White: Associated with being pure, fresh, and good, white's basic feature is equality, implying fairness and impartiality, and reflecting the energies of truth. White urges us to reflect on past transgressions, ours or those of others, not to judge, but to understand, so that we can blossom into our higher selves. The white chrysanthemum represents purity and luck.

Yellow: Although basically a cheerful color, yellow can create feelings of frustration. Babies tend to cry more in yellow rooms. Yellow chrysanthemum represents neglected love or sorrow.

Flower meanings (general): Long life, duplicity, joy and beauty, optimism, everlasting, a wonderful friend, a light of hope in dark times, difficulty, cheerfulness under adversity

Flower message: Keep your chin up. Look at the bright side – there's light at the end of the tunnel.

CLEOME (SPIDER FLOWER)

4 petals
Shape: Spider

Shape meaning: Called "spider flower" because of the long, thread-like stamens that look like a spider's legs. Like a spider, be patient and act only when you are 100% sure that opportunity awaits.

Number meaning: Four evokes a feeling of calmness and solidity. Rooted in the physical world, four tells us to be in the "here and now" and encourages us to build a strong foundation with a down-to-earth perspective.

Color Meanings
Pink: A combination of red and white, pink combines the need for action of red with the insight offered by white to help us succeed.

Purple: Not one of the crowd, purple is unique and independent. Purple seeks originality through creative efforts.

White: Associated with being pure, fresh, and good, white's basic feature is equality, implying fairness and impartiality, and reflecting the energies of truth. White urges us to reflect on past transgressions, ours or those of others, not to judge, but to understand, so that we can blossom into our higher selves.

Flower meanings: Elope with me, I'm not as bad as I seem

Flower message: The time is right to make a decision.

COLEUS

Shape: Oval

Shape meaning: Oval is derived from the Latin word ovum, which means egg. This shape represents rebirth, fertility, and even immortality.

Color meanings

Black: Color of strength and protection. Black can indicate a need for secretiveness.

Green: Puts heart and emotions in balance, helping to see both sides of the equation before making the appropriate decision.

Orange: Social and inviting, orange encourages two-way conversations.

Pink: Puts us in touch with our nurturing side, helping us to show tenderness and kindness with empathy and sensitivity. Pink seeks appreciation, respect, and admiration, and doesn't like to be taken for granted. Loves to hear the words "thank you."

Red: An energizing color, red excites the emotions, boosts enthusiasm, and urges us to take action.

Flower meaning: Arrogance

Flower message: Dispose of any arrogant tendencies as this is preventing you from forging relationships. You have the strength and power to take a new path.

COLUMBINE (AQUILEGIA)

5 petals
Shape: Bell

Shape meaning: The bell shape indicates that guidance from within (our intuition) needs to be grounded and put into practice.

Number meaning: Five is the pivotal number of movement and change. Five is about enjoying life, trying new experiences, and making important choices.

Color meanings

Blue: The shade of the sea and the sky, blue is often described as peaceful, secure, and orderly. The color of trust, blue is thought to induce calm and convey tranquility, helping to instill confidence and inner security.

Pink: Represents sweet and innocent children, or our inner child. Pink symbolizes uncomplicated emotions, inexperience, and naivety, and stands for unconditional love and understanding. Pink can bring back pleasant childhood memories associated with the care and thoughtfulness of a maternal figure.

Purple: Represents wisdom and spirituality. An introspective color, purple allows us to connect with our deeper thoughts and inspires us to reach for our highest ideals.

Red: A strong-willed color, red increases confidence, especially to those who are shy or lacking in willpower, by providing a sense of security and protection against fear and anxiety.

Salmon: Reminds us to safeguard our emotions and not to be overly sensitive.

White: Considered a powerful color in feng shui, white creates a sense of order and efficiency, enabling us to declutter our lives of material items or emotional baggage.

Yellow: Puts emotions aside so thoughts come from the head rather than the heart to help with making decisions. Like a scientist who constantly analyzes and looks methodically at both sides, yellow helps us to focus, study, and recall information.

Flower meanings: Wisdom, strength, pride, fear, caprice, folly, love, foolishness, faith, winning, intellect

Flower message: Relax, don't take things too seriously. You have plenty of time to accomplish what you want to as long as you focus on what matters.

CONEFLOWER (ECHINACEA)

15 to 20 petals
Shape: Circle

Shape meaning: The circle evokes the idea of movement and symbolizes the cycle of time.

Number meaning: The number fifteen is telling us to pay attention to our thoughts and ideas so that we can make much-needed changes in our lives.

Color meanings
Orange: The color of encouragement, orange conveys excitement, warmth, and enthusiasm, keeping us motivated to look on the bright side of life. Orange stimulates action, encouraging us to seek out new activities and adventures.

Pink: Puts us in touch with our nurturing side, helping us to show tenderness and kindness with empathy and sensitivity. Pink seeks appreciation, respect, and admiration, and doesn't like to be taken for granted. Loves to hear the words "thank you."

Purple: Represents the future, imagination, and dreams. Purple stimulates the imagination and encourages creative pursuits.

Yellow: A practical thinker, not a dreamer, yellow loves a challenge, especially a mental one, and will help find new ways of doing things. Yellow stimulates our mental faculties and inspires original thought and inquisitiveness.

Flower meanings: Strength, justice, impartiality, skill, capability

Flower message: Release what is holding you back. When you inventory your strengths, you'll see that you have the capacity for success.

CORAL BELLS (HEUCHERA)

5 petals
Shape: Bell

Shape meaning: The bell shape indicates that guidance from within (our intuition) needs to be grounded and put into practice.

Number meaning: Five is the pivotal number of movement and change. Five is about enjoying life, trying new experiences, and making important choices.

Color meanings
Bronze: Represents the capacity and duty to tolerate a judgment and to repent.

Green: The color of growth and health, green is an emotionally positive color that puts heart and emotions in balance, allowing us to love and nurture ourselves and others unconditionally.

Orange: The color of encouragement, orange conveys excitement, warmth, and enthusiasm, keeping us motivated and helping us to look on the bright side of life. Orange stimulates action, encouraging us to seek out new activities and adventures.

Purple: The color of leadership, purple demands respect and exudes power. Purple is ambitious and confident.

Red: An energizing color, red excites the emotions, boosts enthusiasm, and urges us to take action.

Silver: Believed to be a mirror to the soul, silver helps us to see ourselves as others see us.

Flower meanings: Challenge, scholarship, hard work, dainty pleasures, happy love

Flower message: The only way to overcome challenges is by working hard and using common sense.

COREOPSIS

Shape: Circle

Shape meaning: The circle evokes the idea of movement and symbolizes the cycle of time.

Color Meanings
Gold: Associated with richness in life or spirit, gold enhances the true self and helps us develop our psyche.

Mango: Associated with beauty, like the sunset.

Pink: In color psychology, pink is a sign of hope, a positive color that inspires warm and comforting feelings. Everything will be okay, or "everything will be rosy."

Yellow: Boosts enthusiasm for life. Yellow can increase confidence and optimism by alleviating pressures so that joy can return.

Flower meanings: Love at first sight, always cheerful, good luck in money matters

Flower message: Be positive and good things will come your way.

CROCUS

6 petals
Shape: Cup

Shape meaning: Cups are nurturing and embracing. In tarot cards, the cups can render messages of completion, expansion, abundance, and vibrancy. One's "cup of tea" is an expression that is used to describe something one enjoys or is good at.

Number meaning: We invoke the number six when diplomacy is needed to deal with a sensitive matter. Six will reveal solutions in a calm, unfolding manner.

Color meanings

Blue: The shade of the sea and the sky, blue is often described as peaceful, secure, and orderly. The color of trust, blue is thought to induce calm and convey tranquility, helping to instill confidence, and inner security.

Lavender: Associated with the youthful, untamed growth found in nature during the spring. Because of this association with springtime, lavender encourages us to be optimistic about the beginning of a new stage of life.

Orange: The color of encouragement, orange conveys excitement, warmth, and enthusiasm, keeping us motivated to look on the bright side of life. Orange stimulates action, encouraging us to seek out new activities and adventures.

Purple: Represents wisdom and spirituality. An introspective color, purple allows us to connect with our deeper thoughts and inspires us to reach for high ideals.

Yellow: Boosts enthusiasm for life. Yellow can increase confidence and optimism by alleviating pressures so that joy can return.

White: Considered a powerful color in feng shui, white creates a sense of order and efficiency, enabling us to declutter our lives of material items or emotional baggage.

Flower meanings: Cheerfulness, gladness, youthfulness, mirthfulness, glee

Flower message: This flower has a joyful and uplifting effect. Be optimistic.

DAFFODIL

3 petals
Shape: Trumpet

Shape meaning: The trumpet indicates that news is coming your way.

Number meaning: The spiritual energies of the number three activates positive thoughts, promoting efficacious energies and opportunities.

Color Meanings
Orange: The color of encouragement, orange conveys excitement, warmth, and enthusiasm, keeping us motivated to look on the bright side of life. Orange stimulates action, encouraging us to seek out new activities and adventures.

White: Considered a powerful color in feng shui, white creates a sense of order and efficiency, enabling us to declutter our lives of material items or emotional baggage.

Yellow: A practical thinker, not a dreamer, yellow loves a challenge, especially a mental one, and will help find new ways of doing things. Yellow stimulates our mental faculties and inspires original thought and inquisitiveness.

Flower meanings: Resurrection and rebirth, self-love, new beginnings, respect, gracefulness, creativity, inspiration, renewal and vitality, awareness and inner reflection, memory, forgiveness

Flower message: Like a new spring day, the daffodil's message is uplifting and energizing, a time to celebrate a new beginning. This is a time for clarity of thought. Find a creative outlet for energies.

DAHLIA

8 petals
Shape: Circle

Shape meaning: The circle evokes the idea of movement and symbolizes the cycle of time.

Number meaning: We invoke the number six when diplomacy is needed to deal with a sensitive matter. Six will reveal solutions in a calm, unfolding manner.

Color meanings

Bronze: Intimately related to nature, bronze encourages growth through experience.

Orange: The color of encouragement, orange conveys excitement, warmth, and enthusiasm, keeping us motivated to look on the bright side of life. Orange stimulates action, encouraging us to seek out new activities and adventures.

Pink: Puts us in touch with our nurturing side, helping us to show tenderness and kindness with empathy and sensitivity. Pink seeks appreciation, respect, and admiration and doesn't like to be taken for granted. Loves to hear the words "thank you."

Purple: Assists those seeking the meaning of life and spiritual fulfillment. Purple enhances physic ability but also keeps us grounded.

Red: An energizing color, red excites the emotions, boosts enthusiasm, and urges us to take action.

Yellow: Puts emotions aside so thoughts come from the head rather than the heart to help with making decisions. Like a scientist who constantly analyzes and looks methodically at both sides, yellow helps us to focus, study, and recall information.

Flower meanings: Staying graceful under pressure, commitment, elegance, inner strength, creativity, diversity, betrayal, instability, dishonesty, dignity, gratitude.

Flower message: Seek out new pleasures in life and keep moving through challenges instead of letting them hold you back.

DAISY

24 petals
Shape: Circle

Shape meaning: The circle evokes the idea of movement and symbolizes the cycle of time

Number Meaning: Twenty-four symbolizes practicality, honesty, integrity, responsibility, drive, dependability, and inner wisdom.

Color Meanings

Pink: Represents sweet and innocent children, or our inner child. Pink symbolizes uncomplicated emotions, inexperience, and naivety, and stands for unconditional love and understanding. Pink can bring back pleasant childhood memories associated with the care and thoughtfulness of a maternal figure.

White: Considered a powerful color in feng shui, white creates a sense of order and efficiency, enabling us to declutter our lives of material items or emotional baggage.

Yellow: Represents youth, fun, joy, sunshine, and happy feelings. Yellow is also a symbol of friendship, new beginnings, and happiness.

Flower meanings: Innocence, truth, gentleness, loyal love, youthful beauty, cheerfulness, patience, purity, simplicity, new beginnings, keep a secret

Flower message: Celebrate and appreciate simple things. Bring harmony to your home by cleaning out clutter and making it "fresh as a daisy."

DANDELION

5 petals
Shape: Circle

Shape meaning: The circle evokes the idea of movement and symbolizes the cycle of time.

Number meaning: Five is the pivotal number of movement and change. Five is about enjoying life, trying new experiences, and making important choices.

Color meaning
Yellow: A practical thinker, not a dreamer, yellow loves a challenge, especially a mental one, and will help find new ways of doing things. Yellow stimulates our mental faculties and inspires original thought and inquisitiveness.

Flower meanings: Oracle of time and love, faithfulness, happiness, prophet, wishes come true, ability to rise above life's challenges, intelligence, long lasting happiness, youthful joy

Flower message: Like the dandelion that can survive in difficult conditions, you can rise above life's challenges. Remember the cheerfulness of a sunny summer day when things look bleak.

DELPHINIUM (LARKSPUR)

4 petals
Shape: Dolphin

Shape meaning: Delphinium gets its name from the Greek word "delphis," which means dolphin.

Dolphins are friendly, playful creatures. Pirates believed they offered protection.

Number meaning: Four evokes a feeling of calmness and solidity. Rooted in the physical world, four tells us to be in the "here and now" and encourages us to build a strong foundation with a down-to-earth perspective.

Color meanings
Blue: The shade of the sea and the sky, blue is often described as peaceful, secure, and orderly. The color of trust, blue is thought to induce calm and convey tranquility, helping to instill confidence and inner security.

Pink: In color psychology, pink is a sign of hope, a positive color that inspires warm and comforting feelings. Everything will be okay, or "everything will be rosy."

Purple: Represents wisdom and spirituality. An introspective color, purple allows us to connect with our deeper thoughts and inspires us to reach for high ideals.

White: In color psychology, white represents a new beginning, or a blank canvas. This is the time to seize new opportunities. White is reflective and stimulates openness, growth, and creativity.

Flower meanings: Open heart, ardent attachment, levity, lightness, big-hearted fun, well-being, return of a friend is desired, symbol of infinite possibility, protection against danger, pure heart

Flower message: Anything is possible, so keep reaching for the stars, one step at a time. This is a good time to reach out to someone you've been out of touch with.

FORGET-ME-NOT (MYOSOTIS)

5 petals
Shape: Funnel

Shape meaning: Like the funnel of a tornado, we should sweep away emotional and mental thoughts that hold us back to open the path for clearer communication.

Number meaning: Five is the pivotal number of movement and change. Five is about enjoying life, trying new experiences, and making important choices.

Color meanings
Blue: The shade of the sea and the sky, blue is often described as peaceful, secure and orderly. The color of trust, blue is thought to induce calm and convey tranquility, helping to instill confidence and inner security.

Pink: Represents sweet and innocent children, or our inner child. Pink symbolizes uncomplicated emotions, inexperience, and naivety, and stands for unconditional love and understanding. Pink can bring back pleasant childhood memories associated with the care and thoughtfulness of a maternal figure.

White: The color of protection, white offers a sense of peace and calm, comfort and hope. Surrounding our aura with white light helps to deter negativity and encourages us see beyond surface emotions, entanglements, and fear.

Flower meanings: Don't forget me, memories, true love forever, keepsake flower holding a beloved memory, true love

Flower message: Take time to remember those you love, even if they're still with you right now. Create memories and tell the stories of loved ones who have passed so that new generations will know about them.

FOXGLOVE (DIGITALIS)

5 petals
Shape: Bell

Shape meaning: The bell shape indicates that guidance from within (our intuition) needs to be grounded and put into practice.

Number meaning: Five is the pivotal number of movement and change. Five is about enjoying life, trying new experiences, and making important choices.

Color meanings
Blue: The shade of the sea and the sky, blue is often described as peaceful, secure, and orderly. The color of trust, blue is thought to induce calm and convey tranquility, helping to instill confidence and inner security.

Pink: In color psychology, pink is a sign of hope, a positive color that inspires warm and comforting feelings. Everything will be okay, or "everything will be rosy."

Purple: Represents wisdom and spirituality. An introspective color, purple allows us to connect with our deeper thoughts and inspires us to reach for high ideals.

White: In color psychology, white represents a new beginning, or a blank canvas. Now is the time to seize new opportunities. White is reflective and stimulates openness, growth, and creativity.

Flower meanings: Insincerity, selfish wishes, hypocrisy, falsehood, stateliness, youth, protection

Flower message: Be alert, trust your instincts, and stay grounded. This is a time of active imagination and new opportunities.

FREESIA

8 petals
Shape: Funnel

Shape meaning: Like the funnel of a tornado, we should sweep away emotional and mental thoughts that hold us back to open the path for clearer communication.

Number meaning: Eight is the number of abundance and prosperity. The Universe provides an infinite abundance of energy and resources to fulfill the needs, dreams, and desires we conceive.

Color meanings
Orange: The color of encouragement, orange conveys excitement, warmth, and enthusiasm, keeping us motivated to look on the bright side of life. Orange stimulates action, encouraging us to seek out new activities and adventures.

Pink: Puts us in touch with our nurturing side, helping us to show tenderness and kindness with empathy and sensitivity. Pink seeks appreciation, respect, and admiration, and doesn't like to be taken for granted. Loves to hear the words "thank you."

Purple: Not one of the crowd, purple is unique and independent. Purple seeks originality through creative efforts.

Red: Signifies a pioneering spirit and leadership qualities. Red promotes ambition and encourages us to persevere.

White: The color of protection, white offers a sense of peace and calm, comfort and hope. Surrounding our aura with white light helps to deter negativity and encourages us see beyond surface emotions, entanglements, and fear.

Yellow: Puts emotions aside so thoughts come from the head rather than the heart to help with making decisions. Like a scientist who constantly analyzes and looks methodically at both sides, yellow helps us to focus, study, and recall information.

Flower meanings: Innocence, trust, friendship, reminder that love can be calm as well as passionate, thoughtfulness, sweetness

Flower message: Trust your inner guidance to lead as your path unfolds before you.

GERANIUM

5 petals
Shape: Circle

Shape meaning: The circle evokes the idea of movement and symbolizes the cycle of time.

Number meaning: Five is the pivotal number of movement and change. Five is about enjoying life, trying new experiences, and making important choices.

Color meanings
Orange: The color of encouragement, orange conveys excitement, warmth, and enthusiasm, keeping us motivated to look on the bright side of life. Orange stimulates action, encouraging us to seek out new activities and adventures.

Pink: Creates a calming effect on our emotional energies and can relieve feelings of anger, aggression, and neglect. Pink represents compassion, nurturing, and love and shows tenderness with empathy and sensitivity.

Purple: Represents wisdom and spirituality. An introspective color, purple allows us to connect with our deeper thoughts and inspires us to reach for our highest ideals.

Red: A strong-willed color, red increases confidence, especially to those who are shy or lacking in willpower, by providing a sense of security and protection against fear and anxiety.

White: In color psychology, white represents a new beginning, or a blank canvas. Now is the time to seize new opportunities. White is reflective and stimulates openness, growth, and creativity.

Flower meanings: Fervor, melancholy, esteem, confidence, gentility, true friendship, folly, stupidity, comfort, expected or unexpected meeting, ingenuity, preference, peace of mind

Flower message: Instead of dwelling on past mistakes, look at them as learning experiences. Take advantage of new opportunities when they arise.

GERBERA DAISY

5 petals
Shape: Circle

Shape meaning: The circle evokes the idea of movement and symbolizes the cycle of time.

Number meaning: Five is the pivotal number of movement and change. Five is about enjoying life, trying new experiences, and making important choices.

Color meanings
Orange: The color of encouragement, orange conveys excitement, warmth, and enthusiasm, keeping us motivated to look on the bright side of life. Orange stimulates action, encouraging us to seek out new activities and adventures.

Pink: Represents sweet and innocent children, or our inner child. Pink symbolizes uncomplicated emotions, inexperience, and naivety, and stands for unconditional love and understanding. Pink can bring back pleasant childhood memories associated with the care and thoughtfulness of a maternal figure.

Purple: The color of leadership, purple demands respect and exudes power. Purple is ambitious and confident.

Red: Indicates that we need to be more creative and showy in our endeavors. Red encourages us to move forward. Now may be the time to pursue something we desire.

White: In color psychology, white represents a new beginning, or a blank canvas. Now is the time to seize new opportunities. White is reflective and stimulates openness, growth, and creativity.

Yellow: Represents youth, fun, joy, sunshine and happy feelings. Yellow is also a symbol of friendship, new beginnings, and happiness.

Flower meanings: Cheerfulness, purity, friendship, protection, happiness, the simple beauty of a very happy life

Flower meaning: Celebrate life, treasure friendships. This flower pops with joy and wonderful surprises.

GLADIOLA

3 petals
Shape: Funnel

Shape meaning: Like the funnel of a tornado, we should sweep away emotional and mental thoughts that hold us back to open the path for clearer communication.

Number meaning: The spiritual energies of the number three activates positive thoughts, promoting efficacious energies and opportunities.

Color Meanings

Burgundy: Like red, burgundy can increase our energy, but in a more thoughtful, dignified, and controlled way. Burgundy encourages seriousness in behavior.

Pink: A combination of red and white, pink combines the need for action of red with the insight offered by white to help us succeed.

Red: Indicates that we need to be more creative and showy in our endeavors. Red encourages us to move forward. Now may be the time to pursue something we desire.

White: Considered a powerful color in feng shui, white creates a sense of order and efficiency, enabling us to declutter our lives of material items or emotional baggage.

Yellow: A practical thinker, not a dreamer, yellow loves a challenge, especially a mental one, and will help find new ways of doing things. Yellow stimulates our mental faculties and inspires original thought and inquisitiveness.

Purple: Not one of the crowd, purple is unique and independent. Purple seeks originality through creative efforts.

Flower meanings: Readily armed, strength of character, sincerity, love at first sight, natural grace, remembrance

Flower message: Like a gladiator, don't give up. Reassess where you have been putting your efforts, follow your instincts and reach for higher aspirations.

GOLDEN ASTER (GOLDENROD, SOLIDAGO)

6-13 petals
Shape: Funnel

Shape meaning: Like the funnel of a tornado, we should sweep away emotional and mental thoughts that hold us back to open the path for clearer communication.

Number meaning: We invoke the number six when diplomacy is needed to deal with a sensitive matter. Six will reveal solutions in a calm, unfolding manner.

Color meaning
Yellow: A practical thinker, not a dreamer, yellow loves a challenge, especially a mental one, and will help find new ways of doing things. Yellow stimulates our mental faculties and inspires original thought and inquisitiveness.

Flower meanings: Good fortune, encouragement, success, caution

Flower message: The sunny yellow color stands for creativity and growth and encourages you to pursue projects and dreams. Look for the "gold" in all people and situations. Now is the time to be true to yourself and follow your own path.

HEATHER

4 petals
Shape: Bell

Shape meaning: The bell shape indicates that guidance from within (our intuition) needs to be grounded and put into practice.

Number meaning: Four is a grounded and stable number, much rooted in the physical world. Four is about being present, or living in the "now" and building a strong foundation with a down-to-earth perspective.

Color Meanings

Pink: A combination of red and white, pink combines the need for action of red with the insight offered by white to help us succeed.

Purple: Represents wisdom and spirituality. An introspective color, purple allows us to connect with our deeper thoughts and inspires us to reach for our highest ideals.

Red: A strong-willed color, red increases confidence, especially to those who are shy or lacking in willpower, by providing a sense of security and protection against fear and anxiety.

White: In color psychology, white represents a new beginning, or a blank canvas. Now is the time to seize new opportunities. White is reflective and stimulates openness, growth, and creativity.

Flower meanings: Wishes come true, admiration, loneliness, good luck, protection, solitude

Flower message: Heather is the symbol of good luck. Unexpressed creativity is waiting to unfold. Now is a time to reflect and think about what you want to do.

HELLEBORE

5 petals
Shape: Cup

Shape meaning: Cups are nurturing and embracing. In tarot cards, the cups can render messages of completion, expansion, abundance, and vibrancy. One's "cup of tea" is an expression that is used to describe something one enjoys or is good at.

Number meaning: Five is the pivotal number of movement and change. Five is about enjoying life, trying new experiences, and making important choices.

Color meanings
Black: Absorbs negative energy.

Green: Puts the heart and emotions in balance, helping to see both sides of the equation before making the appropriate decision.

Pink: In color psychology, pink is a sign of hope, a positive color that inspires warm and comforting feelings. Everything will be okay, or "everything will be rosy."

Purple: Combines the stability and integrity of the color blue and the energy of red to promote harmony of the mind and emotions, contributing to mental balance.

Red: A strong-willed color, red increases confidence, especially to those who are shy or lacking in willpower, by providing a sense of security and protection against fear and anxiety.

White: The color of protection, white offers a sense of peace and calm, comfort and hope. Surrounding our aura with white light helps to deter negativity and encourages us see beyond surface emotions, entanglements, and fear.

Yellow: Puts emotions aside so thoughts come from the head rather than the heart to help with making decisions. Like a scientist who constantly analyzes and looks methodically at both sides, yellow helps us to focus, study, and recall information.

Flower meanings: Slander, maliciousness, scandal, magical powers to ward off evil spirits, fate, protection

Flower message: Call on the hellebore's flower energy to overcome troubling situations.

HIBISCUS

5 petals
Shape: Trumpet

Shape meaning: The trumpet indicates that news is coming your way.

Number meaning: The number five represents adventure and freedom, encouraging us to embrace new experiences.

Color meanings

Orange: The color of encouragement, orange conveys excitement, warmth, and enthusiasm, keeping us motivated to look on the bright side of life. Orange stimulates action, encouraging us to seek out new activities and adventures.

Peach: Indicates a need for a little more protection. We shouldn't let our emotions get out of control.

Pink: Represents sweet and innocent children, or our inner child. Pink symbolizes uncomplicated emotions, inexperience, and naivety, and stands for unconditional love and understanding. Pink can bring back pleasant childhood memories associated with the care and thoughtfulness of a maternal figure.

Purple: Represents wisdom and spirituality. An introspective color, purple allows us to connect with our deeper thoughts and inspires us to reach for our highest ideals.

Red: An energizing color, red excites the emotions, boosts enthusiasm, and urges us to take action.

Yellow: Represents youth, fun, joy, sunshine, and happy feelings. Yellow is also a symbol of friendship, new beginnings, and happiness.

Flower meanings: Rare beauty, delicate beauty, seize this opportunity, consumed by love, outward expression of joy and happiness, unity, peace

Flower message: Take advantage of opportunities when they present themselves and find reason to celebrate the simplest joys.

HYACINTH

3 petals
Shape: Bell

Shape meaning: The bell shape indicates that guidance from within (our intuition) needs to be grounded and put into practice.

Number meaning: The spiritual energies of the number three activates positive thoughts, promoting efficacious energies and opportunities.

Color Meanings
Blue: Conservative and predictable, change is difficult for blue. When faced with a new or different idea, blue will analyze, think it over, relate the idea to its past experiences, and then take control and do the right thing.

Purple: The color of leadership, purple demands respect and exudes power. Purple is ambitious and confident.

White: Associated with being pure, fresh and good, white's basic feature is equality, implying fairness and impartiality, and reflecting the energies of truth. White urges us to reflect on past transgressions, ours or those of others, not to judge, but to understand, so that we can blossom into our higher selves.

Flower meanings: Constancy, jealousy, sport, play, rashness, sincerity, forgiveness, compassion

Flower message: The hyacinth flower is a symbol of forgiveness and compassion. Let the past be the past. Don't let anyone hold you back from creating the life you were meant to live.

HYDRANGEA

4 petals
Shape: Cup

Shape meaning: Cups are nurturing and embracing. In tarot cards, the cups can render messages of completion, expansion, abundance, and vibrancy. One's "cup of tea" is an expression that is used to describe something one enjoys or is good at.

Number meaning: Four is a grounded and stable number, much rooted in the physical world. Four is about being present, or living in the "now" and building a strong foundation with a down-to-earth perspective.

Color meanings
Blue: Conservative and predictable, change is difficult for blue. When faced with a new or different idea, blue will analyze, think it over, relate the idea to past experiences, and then take control and make the right decision.

Pink: Represents sweet and innocent children, or our inner child. Pink symbolizes uncomplicated emotions, inexperience, and naivety, and stands for unconditional love and understanding. Pink can bring back pleasant childhood memories associated with the care and thoughtfulness of a maternal figure.

White: In color psychology, white represents a new beginning, or a blank canvas. Now is the time to seize new opportunities. White is reflective and stimulates openness, growth, and creativity.

Flower meanings: Boastfulness, vanity, appreciation of understanding, frigidness, heartlessness, you are cold, hurtful feelings

Flower message: Don't inflate your ego by bragging. Stay humble. Be analytical when making decisions, and seek all the facts to consider.

IRIS

3 petals
Shape: Funnel

Shape meaning: Like the funnel of a tornado, we should sweep away emotional and mental thoughts that hold us back to open the path for clearer communication.

Number meaning: The spiritual energies of the number three activates positive thoughts, promoting efficacious energies and opportunities.

Color meanings

Black: Provides comfort and hides insecurity and lack of confidence. In color psychology, black protects us against emotional stress.

Blue: Good at one-way communication, blue enables us to speak in a manner that encourages people to listen to and learn from what we have to say.

Brown: Reminds us to keep our feet on the ground and use common sense.

Orange: Social and inviting, orange encourages two-way conversations.

Pink: Puts us in touch with our nurturing side, helping us to show tenderness and kindness with empathy and sensitivity. Pink seeks appreciation, respect, and admiration and doesn't like to be taken for granted. Loves to hear the words "thank you."

Purple: The color of leadership, purple demands respect and exudes power. Purple is ambitious and confident.

Red: A strong-willed color, red increases confidence, especially to those who are shy or lacking in willpower, by providing a sense of security and protection against fear and anxiety.

White: In color psychology, white represents a new beginning, or a blank canvas. Now is the time to seize new opportunities. White is reflective and stimulates openness, growth, and creativity.

Yellow: A great communicator, yellow loves to talk and helps with networking.

Flower meanings: Communication, elegance, faith, wisdom, valor, appreciation of friendship, good news, a message, new birth

Flower message: Iris reminds us to be ourselves, but it's ok to shift and change. Approach who you are from different angles. What can you do to make yourself shine? Iris is the symbol of communication and messages.

KANGAROO PAW

6 petals
Shape: Fan

Shape meaning: The fan is symbolic, with the small end representing birth, and the blades symbolizing the many possible paths leading away from the beginning.

Number meaning: We invoke the number six when diplomacy is needed to deal with a sensitive matter. Six will reveal solutions in a calm, unfolding manner.

Color meanings
Apricot: Promotes conversation and social interaction.

Orange: The color of encouragement, orange conveys excitement, warmth, and enthusiasm, keeping us motivated to look on the bright side of life. Orange stimulates action, encouraging us to seek out new activities and adventures.

Pink: Puts us in touch with our nurturing side, helping us to show tenderness and kindness with empathy and sensitivity. Pink seeks appreciation, respect, and admiration, and doesn't like to be taken for granted. Loves to hear the words "thank you."

Red: A strong willed color, red increases confidence, especially to those who are shy or lacking in willpower, by providing a sense of security and protection against fear and anxiety.

Flower meanings: Uniqueness and individuality, power, unequal

Flower message: Tackle challenges in your own, unique way, but don't be afraid to reach out to others for help.

LANTANA

4 petals
Shape: Funnel

Shape meaning: Like the funnel of a tornado, we should sweep away emotional and mental thoughts that hold us back to open the path for clearer communication.

Number meaning: Four evokes a feeling of calmness and solidity. Rooted in the physical world, four tells us to be in the "here and now" and encourages us to build a strong foundation with a down-to-earth perspective.

Color meanings

Orange: The color of encouragement, orange conveys excitement, warmth, and enthusiasm, keeping us motivated to look on the bright side of life. Orange stimulates action, encouraging us to seek out new activities and adventures.

Pink: Puts us in touch with our nurturing side, helping us to show tenderness and kindness with empathy and sensitivity. Pink seeks appreciation, respect, and admiration, and doesn't like to be taken for granted. Loves to hear the words "thank you."

Red: A strong-willed color, red increases confidence, especially to those who are shy or lacking in willpower, by providing a sense of security and protection against fear and anxiety.

White: Considered a powerful color in feng shui, white creates a sense of order and efficiency, enabling us to declutter our lives of material items or emotional baggage.

Yellow: A practical thinker, not a dreamer, yellow loves a challenge, especially a mental one, and will help find new ways of doing things. Yellow stimulates our mental faculties and inspires original thought and inquisitiveness.

Flower meanings: Rigor, breaking old patterns, getting energy moving, space clearing, speaking the truth, strengthening boundaries, strengthening will

Flower message: Stick to your beliefs, but be flexible when trying to accomplish your goals.

LAVENDER

Shape: Bell

Shape meaning: The bell shape indicates that guidance from within (our intuition) needs to be grounded and put into practice.

Color meanings

Pink: In color psychology, pink is a sign of hope, a positive color that inspires warm and comforting feelings. Everything will be okay, or "everything will be rosy."

Purple: Not one of the crowd, purple is unique and independent. Purple seeks originality through creative efforts.

White: In color psychology, white represents a new beginning, or a blank canvas. Now is the time to seize new opportunities. White is reflective and stimulates openness, growth, and creativity.

Flower meanings: Acknowledgment, assiduity (paying close attention to what you are doing or to someone), confession, mistrust, tranquility, higher consciousness, release of energy blockages, easing of tension, calmness, purification, refinement, royalty

Flower message: When you are calm, you can let go of negative energy and open yourself up to new possibilities.

LIATRIS

5 petals
Shape: Funnel

Shape meaning: Like the funnel of a tornado, we should sweep away emotional and mental thoughts that hold us back to open the path for clearer communication.

Number meaning: Five is the pivotal number of movement and change. Five is about enjoying life, trying new experiences, and making important choices.

Color meanings
Pink: A combination of red and white, pink combines the need for action of red with the insight offered by white to help us succeed.

Purple: Represents wisdom and spirituality. An introspective color, purple allows us to connect with our deeper thoughts and inspires us to reach our highest ideals

White: Associated with being pure, fresh, and good, white's basic feature is equality, implying fairness and impartiality, reflecting the energies of truth. White urges us to reflect on past transgressions, ours or those of others, not to judge, but to understand, so that we can blossom into our higher selves.

Flower meaning: Truth

Flower message: Look for the facts, and like a blazing star, share your knowledge. You'll impress and be successful.

LILAC

4 petals
Shape: Funnel

Shape meaning: Like the funnel of a tornado, we should sweep away emotional and mental thoughts that hold us back to open the path for clearer communication.

Number meaning: Four evokes a feeling of calmness and solidity. Rooted in the physical world, four tells us to be in the "here and now" and encourages us to build a strong foundation with a down-to-earth perspective.

Color meanings

Blue: The shade of the sea and the sky, blue is often described as peaceful, secure, and orderly. The color of trust, blue is thought to induce calm and convey tranquility, helping to instill confidence and inner security.

Lilac: Friendly and playful, social and compassionate, lilac likes to live in the moment.

Magenta: Is the color of universal harmony and emotional balance. Magenta contains the passion, power, and energy of red, restrained by the introspection and quiet energy of violet. Magenta promotes compassion, kindness, and cooperation.

Pink: In color psychology, pink is a sign of hope, a positive color that inspires warm and comforting feelings. Everything will be okay, or "everything will be rosy."

Purple: The color of leadership, purple demands respect and exudes power. Purple is ambitious and confident.

Violet: Inspires unconditional and selfless love, devoid of ego, motivating us to be sensitive and compassionate.

White: Associated with being pure, fresh, and good, white's basic feature is equality, implying fairness and impartiality, reflecting the energies of truth. White urges us to reflect on past transgressions, ours or those of others, not to judge, but to understand, so that we can blossom into our higher selves.

Flower meanings: Reminder of our first love, confidence, innocence, fastidiousness, youthful innocence and confidence

Flower message: Lilac's fragrance is strong but light and helps to banish negative energy, which is helpful if you are seeking a breakthrough in your life.

LILY

3 petals
Shape: Trumpet

Shape meaning: The trumpet shape indicates a message is coming your way.

Number meaning: The spiritual energies of the number three activates positive thoughts, promoting efficacious energies and opportunities.

Color meanings
Orange: The color of the extrovert, orange releases the body of spiritual limitations, allowing us the freedom to be ourselves.

Pink: Puts us in touch with our nurturing side, helping us to show tenderness and kindness with empathy and sensitivity. Pink seeks appreciation, respect, and admiration, and doesn't like to be taken for granted. Loves to hear the words "thank you."

Red: Indicates that we need to be more creative and showy in our endeavors. Red encourages us to move forward. Now may be the time to pursue something we desire.

White: In color psychology, white represents a new beginning, or a blank canvas. Now is the time to seize new opportunities. White is reflective and stimulates openness, growth, and creativity.

Yellow: A practical thinker, not a dreamer, yellow loves a challenge, especially a mental one, and will help find new ways of doing things. Yellow stimulates our mental faculties and inspires original thought and inquisitiveness.

Flower meanings: Pride, purity, innocence, strong spiritual associations, faithfulness, majesty, prosperity, abundance, motherhood and rebirth, humility

Flower message: There is no need to blow your own horn, as others will speak of your good actions. Now is the time to make thoughts and dreams a reality as the lily is a sign of success.

LISIANTHUS

Shape: Bell

Shape meaning: The bell shape indicates that guidance from within (our intuition) needs to be grounded and put into practice.

Color meanings
Black: Color of strength and protection. Black can indicate a need for secretiveness.

Brown: Reminds us to keep our feet on the ground, be practical, and apply common sense.

Green: The color of growth and health, green is an emotionally positive color that puts heart and emotions in balance, allowing us to love and nurture ourselves and others unconditionally.

Lavender: Associated with the youthful, untamed growth found in nature during the spring. Because of this association with springtime, lavender encourages us to be optimistic about the beginning of a new stage of life.

Pink: Puts us in touch with our nurturing side, helping us to show tenderness and kindness with empathy and sensitivity. Pink seeks appreciation, respect, and admiration, and doesn't like to be taken for granted. Loves to hear the words "thank you."

White: In color psychology, white represents a new beginning, or a blank canvas. Now is the time to seize new opportunities. White is reflective and stimulates openness, growth, and creativity.

Flower meaning: Outgoing nature, appreciation, thoughts, joining of two people for a lifelong bond, traditional values, rising above hardships, overcoming difficulties

Flower message: Show gratitude to other people, in words as well as gestures. In return your friends will help you meet challenges and attain goals.

LOBELIA (CARDINAL FLOWER)

5 petals (most common)
Shape: Funnel

Shape meaning: Like the funnel of a tornado, we should sweep away emotional and mental thoughts that hold us back to open the path for clearer communication.

Number meaning: Five is the pivotal number of movement and change. Five is about enjoying life, trying new experiences, and making important choices.

Color meanings
Blue: Conservative and predictable, change is difficult for blue. When faced with a new or different idea, blue will analyze, think it over, relate the idea to its past experiences, and then take control and do the right thing.

Red: An energizing color, red excites the emotions, boosts enthusiasm, and urges us to take action.

White: Associated with being pure, fresh, and good, white's basic feature is equality, implying fairness and impartiality, reflecting the energies of truth. White urges us to reflect on past transgressions, ours or those of others, not to judge, but to understand, so that we can blossom into our higher selves.

Yellow: A great communicator, yellow loves to talk and helps with networking.

Flower meanings: Malevolence, distinction, dislike, arrogance

Flower message: Do not feed your ego by thinking ill of others. By looking for goodness, you will grow and succeed.

LUPINE

2 Petals
Shape: Spikes or pointed rods

Shape meaning: Spikes or pointed rods indicats a seeker of the truth, looking for a greater meaning of life.

Number meaning: Two reflects the quiet power of judgment and the need for planning. Two beckons us to choose and encourages partnerships and communication.

Color meanings
Pink: In color psychology, pink is a sign of hope, a positive color that inspires warm and comforting feelings. Everything will be okay, or "everything will be rosy."

Purple: Combines the stability and integrity of the color blue and the energy of red to promote harmony of the mind and emotions, contributing to mental balance.

White: The color of protection, white offers a sense of peace and calm, comfort and hope. Surrounding our aura with white light helps to deter negativity and encourages us see beyond surface emotions, entanglements, and fear.

Yellow: Boosts enthusiasm for life. Yellow can increase confidence and optimism by alleviating pressures so that joy can return.

Flower meaning: Dejection, sorrow, happiness, imagination, voraciousness

Flower message: New opportunities are discovered when you find a way to have a positive outlook.

MARIGOLD OR CALENDULA

13 + petals
Shape: Circle

Shape meaning: The circle evokes the idea of movement and symbolizes the cycle of time.

Number meaning: The number thirteen tells us that the power to manifest our desires resides in our ability to remain positive and focused.

Color meanings
Gold: Associated with richness in life or spirit, gold enhances the true self and helps us develop our psyche. Gold helps us to cope with any task, and upon completion, will showcase our capability.

Orange: Social and inviting, orange encourages two-way conversations.

Red: Signifies a pioneering spirit and leadership qualities. Red promotes ambition and encourages us to persevere.

Yellow: A great communicator, yellow loves to talk and helps with networking.

Flower meaning: Cruelty, grief, jealousy, despair, melancholy, flower of the dead, sacred affection, love, the beauty of warmth of the morning sun, creativity, drive to succeed, desire for wealth

Flower message: The sunny color gives the flower the meaning of optimism and success. If you are having a hard time communicating, learn to do so with warmth to facilitate understanding.

MILLION BELLS (CALIBRACHOA)

5 petals
Shape: Star

Shape meaning: The star encourages us to evaluate ourselves and our lives. We strive to arrive at healthy conclusions so that we can go beyond ourselves and contribute to the larger world in the form of art, writing, political, or humanitarian action.

Number meaning: Five is the pivotal number of movement and change. Five is about enjoying life, trying new experiences, and making important choices.

Color meanings
Blue: Good at one-way communication, blue enables us to speak in a manner that encourages people to listen and learn from what we have to say.

Orange: The color of the extrovert, orange releases the body of spiritual limitations, allowing us the freedom to be ourselves.

Pink: A combination of red and white, pink combines the need for action of red with the insight offered by white to help us succeed.

Purple: Represents wisdom and spirituality. An introspective color, purple allows us to connect with our deeper thoughts and inspires us to reach for our highest ideals.

Red: A strong-willed color, red increases confidence, especially to those who are shy or lacking in willpower, by providing a sense of security and protection against fear and anxiety.

White: Color of protection and encouragement, white offers a sense of peace and calm, comfort and hope, helping to alleviate emotional upsets.

Yellow: A practical thinker, not a dreamer, yellow loves a challenge, especially a mental one, and will help find new ways of doing things. Yellow stimulates our mental faculties and inspires original thought and inquisitiveness.

Flower meaning: Warning

Flower message: Bells represent the mind's ability to tap into the wisdom of our higher conscious. Analyze the situation thoroughly and trust your instincts to find a solution.

NARCISSUS

6 Petals
Shape: Trumpet

Shape meaning: The trumpet indicates that news is coming your way.

Number meaning: We invoke the number six when diplomacy is needed to deal with a sensitive matter. Six will reveal solutions in a calm, unfolding manner.

Color meanings
White: In color psychology, white represents a new beginning, or a blank canvas. Now is the time to seize new opportunities. White is reflective and stimulates openness, growth, and creativity.

Yellow: A great communicator, yellow loves to talk and helps with networking.

Flower meaning: Egotism, vanity, self-love

Flower message: This flower is telling you not to take yourself so seriously. Try to be open to others and their ideas. You may learn something!

NASTURTIUM

5 petals
Shape: Funnel

Shape meaning: Like the funnel of a tornado, we should sweep away emotional and mental thoughts that hold us back to open the path for clearer communication.

Number meaning: Five is the pivotal number of movement and change. Five is about enjoying life, trying new experiences, and making important choices.

Color meanings
Orange: Enthusiastic orange calls for adventure and risk-taking, encouraging us to seek out new activities to enjoy.

Pink: Represents sweet and innocent children, or our inner child. Pink symbolizes uncomplicated emotions, inexperience, and naivety, and stands for unconditional love and understanding. Pink can bring back pleasant childhood memories associated with the care and thoughtfulness of a maternal figure.

Red: A strong-willed color, red increases confidence, especially to those who are shy or lacking in willpower, by providing a sense of security and protection against fear and anxiety.

White: In color psychology, white represents a new beginning, or a blank canvas. Now is the time to seize new opportunities. White is reflective and stimulates openness, growth, and creativity.

Yellow: Represents youth, fun, joy, sunshine, and happy feelings. Yellow is also a symbol of friendship, new beginnings, and happiness.

Flower meanings: Loyalty, patriotism, conquest, jest (twist of the nose), joy, energy, creativity, victory in battle

Flower message: The time is right to add more spice to your life and more flavor for activities. Go for it!

ORCHID

3 Petals
Shape: Star

Shape meaning: The star encourages us to evaluate ourselves and our lives. We strive to arrive at healthy conclusions so that we can go beyond ourselves and contribute to the larger world in the form of art, writing, political, or humanitarian action.

Number meaning: The spiritual energies of the number three activates positive thoughts, promoting efficacious energies and opportunities.

Color meanings

Green: Puts heart and emotions in balance, helping to see both sides of the equation before making the appropriate decision.

Orange: Outgoing and uninhibited, orange releases the body of spiritual limitations and gives us the freedom to be ourselves.

Pink: Creates a calming effect on our emotional energies and can relieve feelings of anger, aggression and neglect. Pink represents compassion, nurturing, and love and shows tenderness with empathy and sensitivity.

Purple: Represents wisdom and spirituality. An introspective color, purple allows us to connect with our deeper thoughts and inspires us to reach for our highest ideals.

Red: An energizing color, red excites the emotions, boosts enthusiasm and urges us to take action.

White: In color psychology, white represents a new beginning, or a blank canvas. Now is the time to seize new opportunities. White is reflective and stimulates openness, growth, and creativity.

Yellow: A practical thinker, not a dreamer, yellow loves a challenge, especially a mental one, and will help find new ways of doing things. Yellow stimulates our mental faculties and inspires original thought and inquisitiveness.

Flower meanings: Mature charm, refined charm, wisdom, thoughtfulness, magnificence, love, ecstasy, beauty, luxury, peace, creativity

Flower message: Always be graceful and hold on to your uniqueness, no matter what. Now is not the time to give up. Push yourself a little further, and keep reaching for the stars.

PANSY

5 petals
Shape: Circle

Shape meaning: The circle evokes the idea of movement and symbolizes the cycle of time.

Number meaning: Five is the pivotal number of movement and change. Five is about enjoying life, trying new experiences, and making important choices.

Color meanings
Blue: Conservative and predictable, change is difficult for blue. When faced with a new or different idea, blue will analyze, think it over, relate the idea to its past experiences, and then take control and do the right thing.

Orange: Enthusiastic orange calls for adventure and risk-taking, encouraging us to seek out new activities to enjoy.

Purple: Represents wisdom and spirituality. An introspective color, purple allows us to connect with our deeper thoughts and inspires us to reach for high ideals.

Red: Indicates that we need to be more creative and showy in our endeavors. Red encourages us to move forward. Now may be the time to pursue something we desire.

White: In color psychology, white represents a new beginning, or a blank canvas. Now is the time to seize new opportunities. White is reflective and stimulates openness, growth, and creativity.

Yellow: Puts emotions aside so thoughts come from the head rather than the heart to help with making decisions. Like a scientist who constantly analyzes and looks methodically at both sides, yellow helps us to focus, study, and recall information.

Flower meaning: Think of me, I share your sentiments, you occupy my thoughts, tender and pleasant thoughts, remembrance, considerations, reflections, free thinkers

Flower message: Pansy is a testimony to the power of thought. This is a time of reflection. Strong impulses suggest action.

PETUNIA

5 petals
Shape: Circle

Shape meaning: The circle evokes the idea of movement and symbolizes the cycle of time.

Number meaning: Five is the pivotal number of movement and change. Five is about enjoying life, trying new experiences, and making important choices.

Color meanings
Black: Can be used to absorb negative energy.

Blue: The shade of the sea and the sky, blue is often described as peaceful, secure and orderly. The color of trust, blue is thought to induce calm and convey tranquility, helping to instill confidence and inner security.

Pink: Creates a calming effect on our emotional energies and can relieve feelings of anger, aggression and neglect. Pink represents compassion, nurturing, and love and shows tenderness with empathy and sensitivity.

Purple: Combines the stability and integrity of the color blue and the energy of red to promote harmony of the mind and emotions, contributing to mental balance.

Red: A strong-willed color, red increases confidence, especially to those who are shy or lacking in willpower, by providing a sense of security and protection against fear and anxiety.

Salmon: Helps us reach a deeper understanding towards our own emotions and personality.

White: Associated with being pure, fresh, and good, white's basic feature is equality, implying fairness and impartiality, reflecting the energies of truth. White urges us to reflect on past transgressions, ours or those of others, not to judge, but to understand, so that we can blossom into our higher selves.

Flower meanings: Resentment, anger, keep your promises, do not despair, your presence soothes me, symbol of not losing hope

Flower message: Now is the time to let go of anger and resentment. Doing so will help you move forward and reach your goals.

PHLOX

5 petals
Shape: Trumpet

Shape meaning: The trumpet indicates that news is coming your way.

Number meaning: Five is the pivotal number of movement and change. Five is about enjoying life, trying new experiences, and making important choices.

Color meanings
Pink: Puts us in touch with our nurturing side, helping us to show tenderness and kindness with empathy and sensitivity. Pink seeks appreciation, respect, and admiration, and doesn't like to be taken for granted. Loves to hear the words "thank you."

Purple: Represents the future, imagination and dreams. Purple stimulates the imagination and encourages creative pursuits.

White: In color psychology, white represents a new beginning, or a blank canvas. Now is the time to seize new opportunities. White is reflective and stimulates openness, growth, and creativity.

Flower meaning: Single-mindedness, unanimity, sweet dreams, friendship, agreement, harmony

Flower message: Now is a good time to pursue goals. Pay attention to dreams and the advice of friends.

POPPY

4-6 petals
Shape: Cup

Shape meaning: Cups are nurturing and embracing. In tarot cards, the cups can render messages of completion, expansion, abundance, and vibrancy. One's "cup of tea" is an expression that is used to describe something one enjoys or is good at.

Number meanings: Four evokes a feeling of calmness, five is a "doing" number, representing faith in action, and six is connected to intuition.

Color meanings

Orange: Social and inviting, orange encourages two-way conversations.

Pink: Creates a calming effect on our emotional energies and can relieve feelings of anger, aggression, and neglect. Pink represents compassion, nurturing, and love and shows tenderness with empathy and sensitivity.

Purple: Assists those seeking the meaning of life and spiritual fulfillment. Purple enhances physic ability while keeping us grounded.

Red: A strong-willed color, red increases confidence, especially to those who are shy or lacking in willpower, by providing a sense of security and protection against fear and anxiety.

White: In color psychology, white represents a new beginning, or a blank canvas. Now is the time to seize new opportunities. White is reflective and stimulates openness, growth, and creativity.

Yellow: Boosts enthusiasm for life. Yellow can increase confidence and optimism by alleviating pressures so that joy can return.

Flower meanings: Extravagance and luxury, death and rebirth, disconnect with a person, restful sleep and recovery, consolation for a loss or death in the family, remembering the fallen of various wars and armed conflicts, a lively imagination, peace in death, beauty and success, message delivered in dreams

Flower message: Develop your own inner peace so that you can get a restful night's sleep. Rest will help cultivate your imagination. Pay attention to your dreams.

QUEEN ANNE'S LACE

5 Petals
Shape: Flat

Shape meaning: The flat shape represents the integration of thoughts and ideas.

Number meaning: Five is the pivotal number of movement and change. Five is about enjoying life, trying new experiences, and making important choices.

Color meaning
White: The color of protection, white offers a sense of peace and calm, comfort and hope. Surrounding our aura with white light helps to deter negativity and encourages us see beyond surface emotions, entanglements, and fear.

Flower meaning: Fantasy, self-reliance, sanctuary, protection, haven, catching one's dreams, steadfast love

Flower message: This flower is offering you a safe haven so that you can pursue goals. Take steps to make day dreams a reality.

RANUNCULUS OR BUTTERCUP

5 petals
Shape: Cup

Shape Meaning: Cups are nurturing and embracing. In tarot cards, the cups can render messages of completion, expansion, abundance, and vibrancy. One's "cup of tea" is an expression that is used to describe something one enjoys or is good at.

Number Meaning: Five is the pivotal number of movement and change. Five is about enjoying life, trying new experiences, and making important choices.

Color Meanings

Orange: The color of encouragement, orange conveys excitement, warmth, and enthusiasm, keeping us motivated to look on the bright side of life. Orange stimulates action, encouraging us to seek out new activities and adventures.

Pink: Puts us in touch with our nurturing side, helping us to show tenderness and kindness with empathy and sensitivity. Pink seeks appreciation, respect, and admiration, and doesn't like to be taken for granted. Loves to hear the words "thank you."

Red: A strong-willed color, red increases confidence, especially to those who are shy or lacking in willpower, by providing a sense of security and protection against fear and anxiety.

White: Considered a powerful color in feng shui, white creates a sense of order and efficiency, enabling us to declutter our lives of material items or emotional baggage.

Yellow: Represents youth, fun, joy, sunshine, and happy feelings. Yellow is also a symbol of friendship, new beginnings, and happiness.

Flower meanings: Ingratitude, childishness, wealth, benevolence, riches, humility, neatness, your charms dazzle me

Flower meaning: The flower essence reminds us that self-worth is an inner state, not something that depends on other people's approval or disapproval. Don't act like a child and be responsible for your actions; only then will you achieve success in your endeavors. Choose words carefully, for they will have greater impact now.

ROSE

5 petals
Shape: Cup

Shape meaning: Cups are nurturing and embracing. In tarot cards, the cups can render messages of completion, expansion, abundance, and vibrancy. One's "cup of tea" is an expression that is used to describe something one enjoys or is good at.

Number meaning: Five is the pivotal number of movement and change. Five is about enjoying life, trying new experiences, and making important choices.

In addition to general flower meanings, the rose's color has a special meaning. Both are given here.

Red: A strong-willed color, red increases confidence, especially to those who are shy or lacking in willpower, by providing a sense of security and protection against fear and anxiety. The red rose represents deep and passionate love, respect, beauty, and passion.

Pink: Puts us in touch with our nurturing side, helping us to show tenderness and kindness with empathy and sensitivity. Pink seeks appreciation, respect, and admiration, and doesn't like to be taken for granted. Loves to hear the words "thank you." A Pink rose represents appreciation of friends and family, perfect happiness, joy, and gratitude.

Dark Pink: Dark pink roses represent gratitude and appreciation.

Light pink: A light pink rose represents grace.

Yellow: Represents youth, fun, joy, sunshine and happy feelings. Yellow is also a symbol of friendship, new beginnings, and happiness. The yellow rose's meanings include infidelity, jealousy, decrease of love (upon better acquaintance), symbol of friendship and caring.

Orange: Social and inviting, orange encourages two-way conversations. Orange roses represent passion, energy, fascination and a message to put energy into relationships.

Peach: Indicates a need for a little more protection. We shouldn't let our emotions get out of control. A peach rose represents modesty.

Salmon: Encourages us to be more outgoing and social. A salmon rose stands for desire and excitement.

White: Associated with being pure, fresh and good, white's basic feature is equality, implying fairness and impartiality, reflecting the energies of truth. White urges us to reflect on past transgressions, ours or those of others, not to judge, but to understand, so that we can blossom into our higher selves. A white rose represents purity and silence and tells us to keep a secret.

Cream: Cream colored roses represent charm and thoughtfulness.

Purple: Represents the future, imagination and dreams. Purple stimulates the imagination and encourages creative pursuits. The purple rose stands for enchantment.

Lavender: Encourages us to daydream and galvanize our creative tendencies. Lavender helps us to be open to new thoughts and ideas. Lavender roses represent enchantment and magic.

Burgundy: Like red, burgundy can increase our energy, but in a more thoughtful, dignified, and controlled way. Burgundy encourages seriousness in behavior. A burgundy rose refers to unconscious beauty.

Green: Green is an emotionally positive color, giving us the ability to love and nurture ourselves and others unconditionally. A green rose means constant rejuvenation of spirit.

Flower meaning, general: Roses are the traditional flower of love.

Flower message: Love is what makes the world go round! Treasure family and friends, and when dealing with those you find obstreperous, think of the saying "Kill them with kindness," and they'll succumb.

SNAPDRAGON

2 petals
Shape: Cup

Shape meaning: Cups are nurturing and embracing. In tarot cards, the cups can render messages of completion, expansion, abundance, and vibrancy. One's "cup of tea" is an expression that is used to describe something one enjoys or is good at.

Number meaning: Two reflects the quiet power of judgment and the need for planning. Two beckons us to choose and encourages partnerships and communication.

Color meanings

Orange: The color of encouragement, orange motivates us to act and seek out new activities, especially those that bring us joy.

Peach: Indicates a need for a little more protection of our emotions. Don't let them get out of control.

Pink: Represents compassion, nurturing, and love. Conveys a sense of safety and even vulnerability.

Purple: The color of leadership, purple demands respect and exudes power. Purple is ambitious and confident.

Red: An energizing color, red excites the emotions, boosts enthusiasm and urges us to take action.

Violet: Inspires unconditional and selfless love, devoid of ego, motivating us to be sensitive and compassionate.

White: Associated with being pure, fresh, and good, white's basic feature is equality, implying fairness and impartiality, reflecting the energies of truth. White urges us to reflect on past transgressions, ours or those of others, not to judge, but to understand, so that we can blossom into our higher selves.

Yellow: A practical thinker, not a dreamer, yellow loves a challenge, especially a mental one, and will help find new ways of doing things. Yellow stimulates our mental faculties and inspires original thought and inquisitiveness.

Flower Meanings: Deception, graciousness, presumption, strength under pressure, pockets are a symbol of magic, inner strength under trying circumstances

Flower Message: Like the hidden pockets of the snapdragon flower, you conceal your inner strength. Be graceful under trying circumstances and stay positive, and you'll come out ahead.

ST. JOHN'S WORT (HYPERICUM)

5 Petals
Shape: Star

Shape meaning: The star encourages us to evaluate ourselves and our lives. We strive to arrive at healthy conclusions so that we can go beyond ourselves and contribute to the larger world in the form of art, writing, political, or humanitarian action.

Number meaning: Five is the pivotal number of movement and change. Five is about enjoying life, trying new experiences, and making important choices.

Color meanings
Green: Puts the heart and emotions in balance, helping to see both sides of the equation before making the appropriate decision.

Peach: Indicates a need for a little more protection of our emotions. Don't let them get out of control.

Red: A strong-willed color, red increases confidence, especially to those who are shy or lacking in willpower, by providing a sense of security and protection against fear and anxiety.

Yellow: A practical thinker, not a dreamer, yellow loves a challenge, especially a mental one, and will help find new ways of doing things. Yellow stimulates our mental faculties and inspires original thought and inquisitiveness.

Flower meanings: Protection, hostility, animosity, superstition, originality, sanctity

Flower message: Look to yourself, not to others, for what you need to do.

STOCK

4 petals
Shape: Cup

Shape meaning: Cups are nurturing and embracing. In tarot cards, the cups can render messages of completion, expansion, abundance, and vibrancy. One's "cup of tea" is an expression that is used to describe something one enjoys or is good at.

Number meaning: Four evokes a feeling of calmness and solidity. Rooted in the physical world, four tells us to be in the "here and now" and encourages us to build a strong foundation with a down-to-earth perspective.

Color meanings

Lilac: Not afraid to go against the crowd, lilac encourages emotional expression. Our true voices are more important than other people's opinions.

Magenta: Is the color of universal harmony and emotional balance. Magenta contains the passion, power, and energy of red, restrained by the introspection and quiet energy of violet. Magenta promotes compassion, kindness, and cooperation.

Pink: In color psychology, pink is a sign of hope, a positive color that inspires warm and comforting feelings. Everything will be okay, or "everything will be rosy."

White: The color of protection, white offers a sense of peace and calm, comfort and hope. Surrounding our aura with white light helps to deter negativity and encourages us see beyond surface emotions, entanglements, and fear.

Yellow: Boosts enthusiasm for life. Yellow can increase confidence and optimism by alleviating pressures so that joy can return.

Flower meaning: Contented life, symbol of a happy life, promptness

Flower message: Enjoy the life you have before it is done. If you're feeling frustrated, take "stock" of the blessings in your life to renew the optimism that will lead to contentment.

SUNFLOWER

Number of Petals: Many
Shape: Circle

Shape meaning: The circle evokes the idea of movement and symbolizes the cycle of time.

Color meanings:
Orange: The color of encouragement, orange conveys excitement, warmth, and enthusiasm, keeping us motivated to look on the bright side of life. Orange stimulates action, encouraging us to seek out new activities and adventures.

Red: A strong-willed color, red increases confidence, especially to those who are shy or lacking in willpower, by providing a sense of security and protection against fear and anxiety.

Yellow: Boosts enthusiasm for life. Yellow can increase confidence and optimism by alleviating pressures so that joy can return.

Flower meanings: False riches, pride, haughtiness, devotion, worship, loyalty, adoration, power, warmth, nourishment

Flower Message: The sunflower is a symbol of endurance and strength, telling you to stand tall and face your challenges.

THISTLE

Shape: Tubular

Shape meaning: The tubular shape indicates a connection between two people, communication.

Color meanings
Blue: The shade of the sea and the sky, is often described as peaceful, secure, and orderly. The color of trust, blue is thought to induce calm and convey tranquility, helping to instill confidence and inner security.

Pink: In color psychology, pink is a sign of hope, a positive color that inspires warm and comforting feelings. Everything will be okay, or "everything will be rosy."

White: We can't hide behind white because it amplifies everything in its way.

Flower meanings: Bravery, devotion, durability, strength and determination, intrusion, austerity, symbol of hard work, nobility of character, suffering

Flower message: When life seems overwhelming, don't hide behind the curtain. You have the strength and determination to persevere.

TULIP

3 petals
Shape: Cup

Shape meaning: Cups are nurturing and embracing. In tarot cards, the cups can render messages of completion, expansion, abundance, and vibrancy. One's "cup of tea" is an expression that is used to describe something one enjoys or is good at.

Number Meaning: Three promises new adventures and the assurance of cooperation from others if you need help. Three symbolizes reward and success in most undertakings.

In addition to general flower meanings, the tulip's color has a special meaning. Both are given here.

Color Meanings

Orange: Social and inviting, orange is the color of the extrovert, exuding happiness and joy, and releasing inhibitions. Orange tulips represent happiness.

Purple: Represents the future, imagination, and dreams. Purple stimulates the imagination and encourages creative pursuits. Purple tulips express admiration for a loved one's accomplishments.

Red: Signifies a pioneering spirit and leadership qualities. Red promotes ambition and encourages us to persevere. Red tulips represent love.

Striped: Striped tulips represents a lover's beautiful eyes.

White: Associated with being pure, fresh, and good, white's basic feature is equality, implying fairness and impartiality, reflecting the energies of truth. White urges us to reflect on past transgressions, ours or those of others, not to judge, but to understand, so that we can blossom into our higher selves. White tulips represent an apology.

Yellow: Relies mostly on itself and prefers not to get emotionally involved. Yellow relates to our ego, self-confidence, how we see ourselves, and how others see us. Yellow tulips represent friendship.

Flower meaning: Wealth and importance, arrogance, passion, perfect love, royalty, paradise on earth, royal and regal nature, abundance, prosperity, indulgence, charity, forgiveness, loyalty, fame

Flower message: You need not strive to impress others. Be yourself – each flower in the garden is different.

VERBENA

5 Petals
Shape: Cup

Shape meaning: The cup shape indicates we are thinking with our hearts instead of our heads, thus reflecting spontaneous responses and habitual reactions to situations.

Number meaning: Five is the pivotal number of movement and change. Five is about enjoying life, trying new experiences, and making important choices.

Color meanings
Blue: Conveys feelings of calm, tranquility, serenity, and peace. Blue instills confidence and inspires feelings of trust.

Pink: Puts us in touch with our nurturing side, helping us to show tenderness and kindness with empathy and sensitivity. Pink seeks appreciation, respect, and admiration, and doesn't like to be taken for granted. Loves to hear the words "thank you."

Purple: Combines the stability and integrity of the color blue with the energy of red to promote harmony of the mind and emotions, contributing to mental balance.

Red: A strong-willed color, red increases confidence, especially to those who are shy or lacking in willpower, by providing a sense of security and protection against fear and anxiety.

White: Color of protection and encouragement, white offers a sense of peace and calm, comfort and hope, helping to alleviate emotional upsets.

Flower meaning: Sensibility, enchantment, pleasantry, request for prayers and well wishes, expression of love, healing, creativity, happiness

Flower message: If you are confused by emotions, turn to friends for guidance. They will help you attain balance in life.

VIOLET, VIOLA

5 Petals
Shape: Circle

Shape meaning: The circle evokes the idea of movement and symbolizes the cycle of time.

Number meaning: Five is the pivotal number of movement and change. Five is about enjoying life, trying new experiences, and making important choices.

Color meanings

Blue: Good at one-way communication, blue enables us to speak in a manner that encourages people to listen to and learn from what we have to say.

Pink: A combination of red and white, pink combines the need for action of red with the insight offered by white to help us succeed.

Purple: Represents wisdom and spirituality. An introspective color, purple allows us to connect with our deeper thoughts and inspires us to reach our highest ideals.

Violet: Inspires unconditional and selfless love, devoid of ego, motivating us to be sensitive and compassionate.

White: In color psychology, white represents a new beginning, or a blank canvas. Now is the time to seize new opportunities. White is reflective and stimulates openness, growth, and creativity.

Yellow: A great communicator, yellow loves to talk and helps with networking.

Flower meaning: Faithfulness, loyalty, watchfulness, modesty, humility

Flower message: Speak like a child, frank but without malice. Don't be afraid to express yourself.

WAX FLOWER (CHAMELAUCIUM)

5 petals
Shape: Star

Shape meaning: The star encourages us to evaluate ourselves and our lives. We strive to arrive at healthy conclusions so that we can go beyond ourselves and contribute to the larger world in the form of art, writing, political, or humanitarian action.

Number meaning: Five is the pivotal number of movement and change. Five is about enjoying life, trying new experiences, and making important choices.

Color meanings
Pink: A combination of red and white, pink combines the need for action of red with the insight offered by white to help us succeed.

Purple: Represents the future, imagination, and dreams. Purple stimulates the imagination and encourages creative pursuits.

White: The color of protection, white offers a sense of peace and calm, comfort and hope. Surrounding our aura with white light helps to deter negativity and encourages us see beyond surface emotions, entanglements, and fear.

Yellow: A practical thinker, not a dreamer, yellow loves a challenge, especially a mental one, and will help find new ways of doing things. Yellow stimulates our mental faculties and inspires original thought and inquisitiveness.

Flower meanings: Happiness in marriage, riches, susceptibility

Flower message: If you want to profit, work hard. As Icarus was warned by his father Daedalus not to go too close to the sun, don't be susceptible to schemes. If something sounds too good to be true, don't buy it.

YARROW (ACHILLEA)

5 flower heads
Shape: Flat

Shape meaning: The flat shape represents the integration of thoughts and ideas.

Number meaning: Five is the pivotal number of movement and change. Five is about enjoying life, trying new experiences, and making important choices.

Color meanings
Orange: Relates to our gut instinct and offers emotional strength during difficult times.

Pink: Creates a calming effect on our emotional energies and can relieve feelings of anger, aggression, and neglect. Pink represents compassion, nurturing, and love and shows tenderness with empathy and sensitivity.

Red: A strong-willed color, red increases confidence, especially to those who are shy or lacking in willpower, by providing a sense of security and protection against fear and anxiety.

White: The color of protection, white offers a sense of peace and calm, comfort and hope. Surrounding our aura with white light helps to deter negativity and encourages us see beyond surface emotions, entanglements, and fear.

Yellow: Puts emotions aside so thoughts come from the head rather than the heart to help with making decisions. Like a scientist who constantly analyzes and looks methodically at both sides, yellow helps us to focus, study, and recall information.

Flower meanings: Magnificent beauty, majesty, modesty, youth and rebirth, victory

Flower message: Focus on the beauty around you. Nature nurtures.

ZINNIA

4-5 Petals
Shape: Circle

Shape meaning: The circle evokes the idea of movement and symbolizes the cycle of time.

Number meanings: Four evokes a feeling of calmness and solidity. Rooted in the physical world, four tells us to be in the "here and now" and encourages us to build a strong foundation with a down-to-earth perspective. Five is the pivotal number of movement and change. Five is about enjoying life, trying new experiences, and making important choices.

Color meanings

Orange: Outgoing and uninhibited, orange releases the body of spiritual limitations and gives us the freedom to be ourselves.

Pink: Puts us in touch with our nurturing side, helping us to show tenderness and kindness with empathy and sensitivity. Pink seeks appreciation, respect, and admiration, and doesn't like to be taken for granted. Loves to hear the words "thank you."

Purple: Represents wisdom and spirituality. An introspective color, purple allows us to connect with our deeper thoughts and inspires us to reach for our highest ideals.

Red: A strong-willed color, red increases confidence, especially to those who are shy or lacking in willpower, by providing a sense of security and protection against fear and anxiety.

Salmon: Encourages us to be more outgoing and social.

White: In color psychology, white represents a new beginning, or a blank canvas. Now is the time to seize new opportunities. White is reflective and stimulates openness, growth, and creativity.

Yellow: Puts emotions aside so thoughts come from the head rather than the heart to help with making decisions. Like a scientist who constantly analyzes and looks methodically at both sides, yellow helps us to focus, study, and recall information.

Flower meanings: Thoughts of absent friends, sincerity, symbol of love

Flower message: If you suddenly think of someone who you've been out of touch with, make contact. You'll be glad you did.

RESOURCES

Alphapedia. "The Bronze Color: Psychology and Meaning. Types and Varieties."

Andrews, Ted. *Nature Speaks – Signs, Omens and Messages in Nature.* Dragonhawk Publishing. March 1, 2004. Jackson, TN. ISBN-13: 9781888767377.

"Arts & Culture." *Plant Profile: Lantana camara,* March 12, 2015.

Ava's Flowers, "Hypericum (Hypericaceae)." 2006-2020 Avas Flowers, https://flowers.avasflowers.net/avasflowers-wiki/hypericum.

Biddy Tarot. "Tarot Card Meanings." *The Meanings of the Suit of Cups,* https://www.biddytarot.com/tarot-card-meaning/minor-arcana/suit-of-cups/.

Bourn, Jennifer. "BournCreative". *Color Meaning: Meaning of the Silver Color,* October 30, 2010, BournCreative, bourncreative.com/meaning-of-the-color-silver/.

Brilliance. "The Meaning of Oval Engagement Rings." Brilliance, LLC, 2000.

Brown, Sharon (Sharran) "Daves Garden." *Goldenrod Legends and Lore,* November 13, 2012, 2020 MH Sub I, LLC dba Internet Brands, davesgarden.com/guides/articles/views/1194.

Caryopsis, Johnny. "Nature North, Manitobas Online Nature Magazine." *The Biology of Dandelions,* naturenorth.com.

Cherry, Kendra and Gans, Steven, MD (medical reviewer). "Cognitive Psychology." *Color Psychology: Does it Affect How You Feel? How Colors Impact Moods, Feelings and Behavior,* May 28, 2020, 2020 About, Inc. (Dotdash), verywellmind.com/color-psychology-2795824.

Chiazzari, Suzy. *Flower Readings: Discover Your True Self with Flowers Through the Ancient Art of Flower Psychometry.* Penguin Random House. 2000. New York, NY. ISBN-10: 0852073380

Connolly, Shane. *The Language of Flowers.* Rizzoli. 2004. New York, NY. ISBN 13: 9780847826056.

Crisp, Tony. "Dreams, health, yoga, body mind & spirit." *Pipe, Tube,*1999-2010, tony Crisp. https://dreamhawk.com/dream-dictionary/pipe-tube/.
"Eagle Spirit Ministry." *The Meaning of Flowers,*" 1996-2020, Tsunyotakohe't, eaglespiritministry.com

Field, Ann, and Scoble, Gretchen. *The Meaning of Herbs: Myth, Language and Lore.* Chronicle Books. May 1, 2001. San Francisco, CA. ISBN 978-0-8118-3071-7 (hc).

Flo, Aunty. "Flower Reading Made Easy!" *Flowers Dictionary: Learn how to predict the future using flowers,* 2020, www.auntyflo.com>flower-dictionary.

"Flower Meanings."*Flowers & Their Meanings,* www.flowermeaning.com.
"FTD by Design". *Lilac Meaning and Symbolism,* June 8, 2016, FTD.com, https://www.ftd.com/blog/share/lilac-meaning-and-symbolism.

Gianni, Annmarie. "AnneMarie Skin Care." *20 Ways to Use Color Therapy to Improve Your Life,* March 23, 2018, annmariegianni.com/20-ways-to-use-color-therapy/.

Green, Imelda."Trusted Psychic Mediums." *The Spider Spirit Animal,* 2020, Trusted Psychic Mediums, trustedpsychicmediums.com/spirit-anims/spider-spirit-animal/.

Haviland-Jones, Jeannette, Hale Rosario, Holly. "Sage Journals." *An Environmental Approach to Positive Emotions: Flowers,* January 1, 2005, journals.sagepub.com/doi/full/10.1177/147470490500300109.

Heilmeyer, Marina. *The Language of Flowers (Art and Design).* Prestel Publishing. April 1, 2001. New York, NY. ISBN 13: 9783791323691.

Hunter, Candace. "The Practical Herbalist." *St. John's Wort: Sunny Weed with a History,* The Practical Herbalist Design and customization by Mud Paw Design House, https://www.thepractcalherbalist.com/author/raven14/

Kaminski, Patricia. "Flower Essence Society." *Saint John's Wart,* The Flower Essence Society, The Flower Essence Society, flowersociety.org/SJW.htm.

Kasamba Staff. "Tarot Card: The Star, Major Arcana XVII." *Insight from a Kasamba Tarot Reader,* 2019, Kasamba. com, kasamba.com/tarot-reading/decks/ajor-arcana/the-star-card/.

King, Bernadette. "Building Beautiful Souls." *Thistle,"* 2020 Building Beautiful Souls, Inc.

Kirby, Mandy. *A Victorian Flower Dictionary: The Language of Flowers Companion.* Random House. September 11, 2011. New York, NY. Group, 2011.

Lizzy. "Chakras Info." *The Throat Chakra,* December 24, 2019, 2020,Chakras.info, https://www.chakras.info/throat-chakra/.

Love, Presley. "Flower Symbolism & Spiritual Meaning of Flowers." *Universe of Symbolism, Universe* of Symbolism, 2020, universeofsymbolism.com/flowers.symbolism.html.

Loy, Susan. *Flowers, the Alphabet: The Language and Poetry of Flowers.* CSL Press. January 1, 2001. Moneta, VA. ISBN10: 0970211317. ISBN 13: 9780970211316.

"Minnesota Wildflowers, A Field Guide to the Flora of Minnesota." *Echinacea angustifolia,* 2006-2020, www.minnesotawildflowers.info/flower/eastern-purple-coneflower.

"Minnesota Wildflowers: a field guide to the flora of Minnesota." *Solidago rigida (Stiff Goldenrod),* 2006-2020, MinnesotaWildflowers, minnesotawildflowers.info/flower/stiff-goldenrod.

Venefica, Avia. "Taro Teaching.com – Shedding Light on Taro Wisdom." 2007-2018, Avia Venefica.www.tarotteachings.com, minnesotawildflowers.info/flower/stiff-goldenrod.

Olsen, Jacob. "Color Meanings." *Color Symbolism – What Do Colors Symbolize?*2020, About Color Meanings, color-meanings.com/color-symbolism-what-do-colors-symbolize/.

Native Indian Tribes. "Native American Symbols." *The Arrow Symbol*, 01-16.-2008, 2017 Siteseen Limited, https://www.warpaths2peacepipes.com/native-american-symbols/arrow-symbol.htm.

New Bedford Whaling Museum. "Japanese Culture and the Use of Fans." August 7, 2015, 2011-2020 ODHS/New Bedford Whaling Museum, https://www.whalingmuseum.org/online exhibits/fans/fashion.html.

Pickles, Sheila (Editor). *The Language of Flowers: Penhaligon's Scented Treasury of Verse and Prose*. Harmony Books. December 30, 1989. ISBN 10: 0517574608. ISBN 13: 9780517574607.

Scott-Kemmis, Judy. "Empowered by Color." *Understanding the Meaning of Colors in Color Psychology*, 2009-2018, Copyscape, empower-yourself-with-color-psychology.com/meaning-of-colors.

Stephens, Siva. "Classroom." *Symbolism of Japanese Fans*, 2001-2020, Leaf Group Ltd., https://classroom. Synonym.com/symbolism-of-japanese-fans-12080856. html.

Sweet Dreams: we know all about dreams. "The meaning of the dream symbol: Ball." 2015-2017, We Know all About Dreams, weknowyourdreams.com.

"Teleflora." *Discover the Language & Meanings of Flowers/ Teleflora*, www.teleflora.com>meaning-of-flowers.

"Teleflora." *The Symbolism of Flower Colors is Steeped in Tradition*, teleflora.com/floral-facts/flower-color-meaning.

Throat Chakra – Visuddha. "Throat Chakra at a glance: Throat Chakra Affirmations." 2011—2020, Copyscape, chakra-anatomy.com/throat-chakra.html.

Whitehurst, Tess. "Live Your Magic." *Lantana (Shrub Verbena)*.

"What's in Your Dream? Dream Moods." http://www.dreammoods.com/dreamthemes/colors-dream-symbols.htm.

"Wikipedia The Free Encyclopedia." Solidago, March 20, 2020.

Wyatt, Nikki. "Spirit of Transformation." *St. John's Wort: Finding the Source of Our Light Within, Releasing Karmis Fear – Finding protection*, spiritoftransformation.com/essencesdescriptions/stjohnswort.pdf.